THE CHURCH, THE SOUTH AND THE FUTURE

THE CHURCH,
THE SOUTH
AND THE FUTURE

by
James J. Thompson, Jr.

Christian Classics, Inc.
WESTMINSTER, MD 21157
1988

First published 1988
©1988 by James J. Thompson, Jr.
ISBN: 0-87061-165-8
Library of Congress Catalog Card: 88-062556
Printed in the United States of America

To

FATHER ANTHONY J. WARNER
AND
SHELDON VANAUKEN,
Catholics *and* Virginians

Contents

Preface ix

I. New South, Old Religion 1

II. The Pope's Folks in the Land of
    Cotton 23

III. Catholic-Baiting with a Southern
     Accent 43

IV. It's a Long, Hard Road from Dixieland to
     Rome 69

V. If Your Heart's Not in Dixie 95

VI. A Catholic South? 115

Debts and Acknowledgements 127

Preface

I became a Southerner in 1944 when I was born on a farm in Maryland to a mother whose people had settled the area before the Revolution; my father's family claimed equal longevity in neighboring Virginia. I became a Catholic in 1975 when I converted to the Church. Since then, two compelling identities have competed for my loyalty. "Catholic Southerner": Is this an oxymoron?

I did not cook up this conflict on my own. Many Southern Protestants have long been convinced that no true son of the South could be a Catholic, for Protestantism forms an essential ingredient of Southernness. American Catholics are often wary of Southerners, spying in them the marks of a rancorous anti-Catholicism.

The editor of the *Tennessee Register*, the Nashville diocese's weekly paper, recently chastised white Southerners for their attachment to the song "Dixie." Although the editor is a native Southerner, he finds the song repellent. Urging that it be banished to museum archives, he concludes: "But I do not like to think that we have that much in common with those times 125 years ago and with the 'fields of cotton'. God grant that we do not." Well, *I* do; I am proud of it, and it has nothing to do with slavery or racial subjugation. It involves love of one's ancestors and humility in the face of their efforts to live as decent and honorable people. I do not intend to repudiate "Dixie"; does this make me a bad Catholic?

I hope the following pages will illuminate this matter of conflicting identities, both as it existed in the past and as it survives in the present. I have not completely resolved the dilemma to my own satisfaction; I doubt that I ever shall. I know only that I love both the Church and my native land, and I will not choose between them for the sake of inner harmony. This book is not a work of historical scholarship nor of sociological analysis. It is simply one Catholic Southerner's reflections on his region and his Church.

Chapter I appeared in slightly different form in the *New Oxford Review*, LV (June 1988), 5-14. I thank Dale Vree, the editor, for permission to reprint this material.

1. New South, Old Religion

Back in the old days, before the South underwent sunbel-
tization, Yankees ventured into Dixie with trepidation.
Racing through the former Confederacy on their way to the
sun-blanched splendors of Florida, they peered from their
fancy automobiles at a people and landscape filled with mi-
natory portents. Those ragged Negroes, slack-jawed rednecks,
scraggly hound dogs, battered pickup trucks, fetid swamps
and languid, muddy rivers sent a prickling of fear crawling
down the Yankee spine. It was all so . . . well, *Faulknerian*.
Beneath its sluggish and placid surface it seethed with the
dreadful and unspeakable: homicide, insanity, imbecility, in-
cest, miscegenation. When it involved the South, the Yankee's
legendary sangfroid and unblinking realism succumbed to the
phantasmal.

That has changed. The South, once condemned as a stag-
nant backwater—an embarrassment to wholesome, energetic
Americans—has undergone a metamorphosis in the popular
mind. The alluring image of the Sun Belt has banished the
phantasmagoria of the past. Tobacco Road has been transformed into an Atlanta suburb: "Tara Estates"; Jeeter Lester's
grandson, J. Lester III, commutes by BMW to his brokerage
firm on Peachtree Street. Bustling entrepreneurs have shouldered aside the fabled Good Ole Boy—he of tobacco wad, beer

1

can, shotgun and demented, toothless grin. Formerly wedded
to the past, the South pulsates with progress and scintillant
visions of the future. Once not fully American, it embodies the
quintessence of Americanism. The Yankee no longer experiences the old surge of foreboding and revulsion as he speeds
toward Florida; instead he mulls the possibility of abandon-
ing a decrepit Rust Belt to try his luck in Dixie. In the late
twentieth century the South is, as they like to say in the board-
rooms and promethean towers, where the action is.

II

Imagine a Northern friend (yes, "friend": the war is over
and he exudes amiability) on a leisurely foray into the South.
He has crossed its borders this time without a Florida tan in
mind; he comes now as a prospective migrant. Business has
sagged in his native Pennsylvania, and he is pondering a relo-
cation to Nashville, a city that burbles with Sun Belt efferves-
cence. The Northerner spends Saturday in an unhurried drive
through the Shenandoah Valley on Interstate 81. The Virginia
landscape at its most ravishing unfolds before his eyes as he
consumes the miles from Winchester southward. Late Saturday afternoon he exits at Bristol on the Tennessee border,
checks into a sparkling Sheraton Inn (spiffier than the super-
annuated one at home), and relaxes over a sumptious meal at
a well-appointed steak house. (No grits or red-eye gravy on
this menu.) Back in his hotel room he retires to a night of
easeful sleep. As he drifts off, he hums "Dixie" and dreams of
the dollars that sprout as thickly in the southland as tobacco
and cotton once did.

The next morning he continues toward Nashville, a
five-hour drive across East Tennessee. He reaches for the radio knob, seeking music to complement his expansive mood.
The soporific hum of motor and tire yields to a choir singing
"What a Friend We Have in Jesus." The Northerner smiles;

why, it's Sunday morning: Southerners take their religion more seriously than do folks in the Northeast. He, too, believes in God, and he even recognizes the hymn from his youthful Sunday School days, but he wants an E-Z-listening station. He turns the dial: hideous nasal voices moan a gospel song, something about Jesus, Mama, heaven and death. Ah, well, try again: a raucous black choir shouts "Hallejulah!" and "Praise Jesus!" Our Northerner is an enlightened man—no racist—and he is fond of black music, but by "black music" he means the Temptations, Lionel Richey or Whitney Houston. Irritated, he twirls the dial: a Jesus-screaming preacher caterwauls about sin, Satan, damnation and hell-fire. My God, the Northerner mutters, as he urgently twists the knob. Another ranter's voice blasts from the radio; this one is discernibly black, but no less unpalatable. He snaps off the radio in disgust.

Disquietude creeps upon our visitor, souring the contentment that has sweetened his journey till now. He grumbles at the South's devotion to retrograde religion. Disagreeable images assault his brain. The Sun Belt exudes dollars and dynamism, but, he recalls, it also boasts Pat Robertson, Jerry Falwell, Jimmy Swaggart and that bevy of odious tv evangelists. These Southerners scream the loudest about secular humanism and they ban books and probably burn them as well. They thumb their nose at the law and clamor for prayer in the public schools. And who leads the campaign against the teaching of evolution? Southerners! East Tennessee-Dayton-the Scopes trial: the Northerner chuckles as he remembers Mencken's ripostes at the "gaping primates" of the South. But it's not funny: they still exist! And snake-handlers! He shudders: East Tennessee probably abounds with crazed fools with rattlesnakes draped around their neck!

Greatly shaken, our Northern friend finally arrives in Nashville. The sleek office towers, sprawling condo complexes and gilded shopping malls reassure him that he has returned to civilization, but the fiasco with the radio has left him disconcerted. How deep does the Sun Belt ethos penetrate? Is it nothing more than a veneer that barely conceals a South still replete with snake-handlers, frenzied faith-healers, ignorant evangelists, lynchers, moonshiners, rednecks and drooling cretins who sleep with their sisters? Is Nashville—apparently a locus of Sun Belt boosterism—still at heart the buckle on the Bible Belt? Our Northerner thinks twice, thrice: Does he belong in the South?

III

That is a complex question, the answer to which illustrates the South's notorious genius for perplexing outsiders by piling paradox upon paradox and combining wildly disparate elements into a whole that defies facile categorization. Is the South still the Bible Belt? Well, yes—but then, no, too: at least not in precisely the same way that it used to be. Of one thing our Northerner can be certain: the Sun Belt exists; it was not cooked up in the calculating brain of a Madison Avenue or Peachtree Street ad-man.

Today's Southerner is a man of the present and future. He no longer caressingly polishes his great-great-granddaddy's sword; nor does he hear in his mind the rattle and beat of musket fire at Cemetery Ridge or Lookout Mountain, nor catch the faint echo of horses' hooves at Brandy Station or Spotsylvania Court House. No longer is he a one-gallused farmer who dribbles tobacco juice down his chin and snatches up rope and faggot to teach "uppity niggers" their place. Today's Southerner is increasingly a middle-class suburbanite, brother under the skin to his counterparts in Boston, Philadelphia, Cleveland, Chicago and Los Angeles. He is patriotic, prosperous, optimistic and happy to be part of the burgeoning Sun Belt; he even gravitates toward the Republican party. He is, in short, exactly what our Northern visitor expects (and wants) to find in Richmond, Charlotte, Columbia, Atlanta, Birmingham, Nashville, Memphis and the other vibrant cities that prosyletize for the "New South." But he is also religious, and there's the rub for the Northerner.

IV

Religion as such is not exotic to our visitor. His native Northeast boasts a population overwhelmingly agreed upon the proposition that God exists. As Mr. Gallup regularly affirms, brazenfaced atheists are as scarce in the United States as Mormon existentialists in Salt Lake City. To acknowledge belief in God's existence reveals little of one's faith and commitment. This "god" can be as vague as the philosopher's Prime Mover or the Enlightenment's Great Clockmaker. The South's religiosity involves far greater specificity. Southerners attend church more often than do other Americans; they more eagerly declare their reliance upon a "personal Savior"; and they more frequently confess that God plays an intimate and determining role in their life. According to recent polls, almost half of those Americans who claim to be "born again" live in the South.

A Southerner assumes not only that his neighbors are Christians, but he takes it for granted that they belong to a particular denomination. Southerners rarely refer to themselves merely as "Christians"; the denominational tag takes precedence. Although the distinctions may be unfathomable to a Northerner, it matters in the South whether one is an independent Baptist or Convention Baptist, a Cumberland Presbyterian or a plain old Presbyterian, a Disciple of Christ or a member of the Church of Christ. (The latter two are distinguished as "fiddlin' Campbellites" and "non-fiddlin' Campbellites" in recognition of their mutually exclusive teachings on the role of musical instruments in worship services.) Even those who no longer attend church continue to identify with the faith of their upbringing. When asked what church he belongs to, a man who has not darkened the door of a house of worship in twenty-five years will answer (with memories of Sunday School, Bible stories and his sainted Mama): "Baptist," "Methodist" or whatever. In the South only politics and college football rival religion in the loyalty they evoke and the passions they inflame.

The bulk of Southerners, black and white alike, are either Baptists or Methodists. A familiar quip: There are more Baptists and Methodists in the South than people. Presbyterians and Episcopalians have their place, but folks in those churches boast more money and social prestige than numbers. The South—especially Texas and Tennessee—claims the lion's share of a denomination little known outside the region: the Church of Christ, a Bible-believing army of hard-bitten fundamentalists (*never* to be confused with the United Church of Christ, a Bible-ignoring regiment of equally hard-bitten liberals in the North). Beyond these faiths, one finds a plethora of pentecostals, independent fundamentalists and adherents of the more *outré* sects. Unitarians, Christian Scientists, Quakers and other votaries of liberal Protestantism are scarce. Nor does the region harbor significant numbers of those affiliated with what the Southerner calls "ethnic" churches: Lutheran, Roman Catholic and Eastern Orthodox.

Not only is the South overwhelmingly Protestant, but it is predominantly fundamentalist. This faith places little premium upon many of the characteristic features of historic Christianity. Neither sacramentalism nor liturgy nor theology plays a major role in the Southerner's religious life. The foundation stone of his faith is the Bible, a book he professes to read literally. "Bible-believing" (as in "Bible-believing Baptist") is a popular and honorable epithet in the South.

In his church services the Southerner demands florid, dramatic preaching and lusty and loud congregational singing. He insists on emotional warmth, on a religion of the heart that expresses itself in everything from the decorous tears of a Methodist to the ecstatic babblings of those seized by the

Spirit. He speaks of "knowing Jesus," of "having a personal relationship with the Savior," of living on intimate terms with the deity. He believes in sin, salvation, heaven and hell in a graphic and literal way, and the cool rationality of liberal Protestantism strikes him as a species of unbelief. I once asked a friend of mine why he always capitalized the word "heaven." Surprised by my opacity, he answered testily: "Why, because it's the proper name of a *place,* just as surely as is Cleveland or Boston or Los Angeles." And heaven, I should add, is far more real to my friend than any of these cities. The Southerner's faith directs him toward salvation of the individual soul and away from a corporate sense of communal religious endeavor. The Social Gospel, with its emphasis upon societal improvement, has never caught on in the South.

To live in the South is to be acutely aware of religion's presence. Even what some observers have called the "Americanization of Dixie" has not altered this. The Sun Belt entrepreneur flourishes in the secular milieu of high finance, but he retains a measure of respect for the faith of his fathers, even if he no longer practices it rigorously. The completely secularized individual, not uncommon in the North, is a rarity in the South.

Flannery O'Connor once remarked that though the Southerner may not be "Christ-centered," he is assuredly "Christ-haunted." Money, social mobility and improved education have not lessened this haunting in the thirty or so years since O'Connor ventured her observation. To put it more prosaically: the Southerner dwells in a culture and society drenched in religion. It may soar to the sublime or wallow in the ridiculous, but in whatever shape, religion is indubitably *there.*

V

One of its most obvious manifestations is the ubiquitous clergyman, invariably called a "preacher." In the rural and small-town South (which most of the region remained until the 1950s) two personages historically commanded highest respect: the lawyer and the preacher. The first supervised the realm of politics, the other the sacred precincts, and politics and religion have formed the core of Southern life. To host the preacher at Sunday dinner is an occasion of lofty honor; generations of Southern cooks have lavished their culinary talents on meals that would leave him dizzy with contentment.

The preacher presides over the most solemn and joyful rites of passage: baptism, marriage, death. Funerals of even the most egregious reprobates are conducted by a man of the cloth. In a Christ-haunted land one does not take chances when confronted with the Ultimate Question. The preacher may be forced to speak of the deceased in the vaguest terms, and he may have to stretch the limits of credulity to find something good to say about the old miscreant, but the proper obsequies will be offered. Southerners dutifully invite the preacher's advice and counsel; Northerners turn to psychiatrists, Southerners consult practitioners of a more ancient faith. The wise Southern politician keeps an ear cocked toward the preachers; on many issues, as goes the pulpit, so goes the pew.

This does not mean that the South groans under clerical tyranny. Southerners, especially Baptists, are touchy about strict separation of church and state, and a preacher had best be sensitive to the boundaries of his influence. "Pray, pay and obey," a slogan applied to pre-Vatican II Catholics, does not set well in the South. A preacher cannot wield the power of the sacraments to force a recalcitrant congregant into line. Should a Baptist preacher (or most any kind, since most of the South's churches are largely congregational in polity) overstep his approved authority, the congregation will toss him out and call a more agreeable parson to the pulpit. The preacher is the shepherd, the congregation the flock, but these sheep can be decidedly wolf-like at times.

The centrality of the clergyman appears in the richness and profusion of preacher jokes. Three subjects account for most Southern humor: hunting, race (black jokes about whites, as well as vice versa) and religion. The preacher is often the butt of these tales, but the humor seldom stoops to cruelty or bitterness. Rather it arises from fondness and a lighthearted refusal to take the preacher quite as seriously as he might wish.

Since a Southerner never passes up the opportunity to regale an audience with a good story, I offer several examples of the genre. I shall resist the temptation to analyze, that being the task of humorless sociologists, psychologists and anthropologists. As Wordsworth warned, to dissect is to murder.

A farmer is working in a distant field. His small son comes racing across the furrows, excitedly shouting: "Daddy! Daddy! There's a preacher up at the house!" "What kind of preacher?" asks the father. "I don't rightly know," replies the boy, "but it sure is a preacher." The farmer pauses, slowly wipes his brow with a large bandana, and says: "Son, I'll be up to the house directly, but I want you to run back as fast as you can and find out what kind of preacher it is. If it's an Episcopal one, you plant yourself in front of the cupboard where I keep my whiskey. If he's a Methodist, stand in front of the ice box. But if it's a Baptist preacher, you crawl up on your Mama's lap and don't move till I get there."

Three preachers—a Baptist, a Methodist and an Episcopalian—and their wives all die at the same time and present themselves before St. Peter for admission into heaven. St. Peter questions each in turn to determine their worthiness. First to the Episcopalian: "Well, Reverend Carrington, I see you and the missus want to enter the pearly gates. By the way, what is your wife's name?" "Brandy," the parson answers. "Good Lord!" shouts St. Peter, "you Episcopalians think about nothing but drinking. Get out of here; we don't want any drunks." The Methodist preacher and his wife step forward. St. Peter: "Greetings, Preacher Brown, and what is your wife's name?" Cautiously the preacher replies: "Penny." "Oh, no," groans St. Peter, "you Methodists are obsessed with money. We don't need any misers up here." The Baptist has been watching with growing alarm. With the dismissal of his Methodist colleague, he turns to his wife and says: "Come on, Fanny, we might as well leave right now."

I shall burden the reader with one more; after all, this furthers the enterprise of serious cultural analysis. Three preachers—a Methodist, a Baptist and, for variety's sake, a Presbyterian—decide to indulge in a day of fishing. Armed with poles and bait they climb into a boat and row a piece out into a lake. When the boat stops the Methodist suddenly says: "Shucks, I left my lunch bucket on shore. I'll be right back." He clambers over the side of the boat, walks across the surface of the water, picks up his lunch, walks back and resumes his seat in the boat. The Baptist preacher is speechless, but he conceals his amazement from his nonchalant colleagues. A short time passes. The Presbyterian slaps the back of his neck. "Doggone pesky mosquitoes! I'll be right back; I'm going to get some insect spray from the car." With studied casualness he repeats the performance made earlier by the Methodist. The Baptist's mouth gapes open. By God, he says to himself, if they can do it so can I. With that, he announces: "I forgot something; I'll be back in a minute." He steps over the side of the boat and immediately plunges beneath the water. The Methodist looks at the Presbyterian and grins: "Do you think we should have told him about those rocks?"

VI

The Southerner is apt to confuse religion with morality. Granted, the two are related; the problem is that the Southerner frequently defines morality narrowly and substitutes his constricted morals for the liberating gospel of Christ. At its worst, this pinching moralism compels the fundamentalist to proscribe everything that offers fleshly delight. H. L. Mencken's definition is apposite: a Puritan is a person who fears that someone may be having fun. This tendency lends to

Southern religion a stern, prohibitory visage. Among the most intractable pentecostals, Baptists and adherents of the Church of Christ the list of taboos is long and arduous: alcohol, tobacco, dancing, card playing, worldly music (defined as anything not fit for the ears of your grandmother), mixed-gender swimming, movies, jewelry, make-up, "provocative" female attire (read: shorts and low-cut or high-rise dresses), and anything else that would distract the believer's attention from the strait way to heaven. The mainstream denominations generally differ from this mentality in degree rather than kind, save the Episcopalians who, with aristocratic insouciance, indulge in such pagan customs as drinking. For this reason, they are frequently called "Whiskeypalians." Whatever the fundamentalist's heaven may be like, surely he has established his hell on earth.

The difficulty arises when this mentality spills into the public realm. Not only does the fundamentalist mortify his own flesh, but his world-blasting morality compels him to insist that everyone else do so too. The changes that have swept the South since World War Two—greater cultural and social sophistication, urbanization, the influx of Northerners—have brought fundamentalists roaring into the public arena to stanch the hemorrhaging of moral rectitude.

Most commonly this takes the form of a crusade to prevent the sale of liquor by the drink. The battle has already been lost in the larger cities—even in cities smaller and less cosmopolitan. A Church of Christ preacher from Memphis once told me, as he ruefully shook his head: "Memphis is a pagan city." I agreed that this might be true, but why, I asked, did he think so? Fixing me with the baleful glare of a Tennessee Savonarola, he spat out the words: "Liquor by the drink. Ever since the law passed, Memphis has been wallowing in filth and iniquity." Feeling the need for a drink, I sidled away and headed for a bar.

The real rub for the fundamentalist is not liquor by the drink; he yearns to banish alcohol altogether. "Get rid of

Satan's brew! Smash the bottles, burn down the liquor stores, return decency to the South!" The prohibitionist entertains no doubt that he speaks the voice of God in urging the expunction of drinking. Such certitude is not to be sniffed at, even by the ungodly. A number of years ago a town in the mountains of Virginia suffered a wrenching debate over a proposal by the state to open a liquor store in the town. (Virginia practices socialism in the sale of hard liquor.) The preachers railed against the pernicious scheme to no avail; the store opened. Falling back on their ultimate weapon, the men of God predicted a rain of divine wrath upon the town. Soon after the store opened, a gasoline tank-truck stalled while crossing the railroad tracks that run through the center of town. A train smashed into the truck, creating a holocaust that consumed the nearby liquor store. The preachers were smug, the drinkers meekly silent; the state refrained from replacing the gutted store.

Demon rum got embroiled in Nashville's mayoral contest in the summer of 1987. One by one the entrants in the Democratic primary swore that ne'er a drop of the vile liquid touched his lips. Two of the candidates admitted—in good fundamentalist confessional fashion—that they had once succumbed to the lure of alcohol, but, having fallen prey to the stuff, they had triumphed over it to lead a life of unsullied abstinence. Only one man had the courage to avow that, as he put it, he liked a glass of wine with dinner. This flagrant boozer, a newcomer from Massachusetts and not attuned to the subtleties of Southern morality, did not realize how grossly he had offended local sensibilities. To godly folk, confession of former drunkenness is acceptable—even admirable—but to admit that one drinks wine with dinner—shamelessly washes down the greens, grits and fried ham with alcohol—is to mark oneself an irredeemable reprobate.

In Tennessee the normal obsession with liquor has temporarily been displaced by a boiling controversy over parimutuel betting. For years the state's horsey set has lobbied legislators to permit betting on thoroughbred racing. Politicians, snuffling around for new sources of revenue, finally realized that horse racing means increased tax monies. State pride figures as well, for Tennesseans begrudge Kentucky's primacy in anything, and the neighbor to the north has long boasted the glories of the Kentucky Derby. Even worse, Alabama recently legalized pari-mutuel betting, and if Tennesseans evince a mild distaste for Kentucky, they consider Alabama beneath contempt. (Among Tennessee's neighbors, only Arkansas ranks lower in esteem.) The legislature voted to permit local referenda on the issue.

Because of Nashville's size, its popularity with tourists, and the presence of horse-raising in the area, the city is a natural site for a race track. Proponents pushed hard for voter approval. But the sin-busters—in this case, a number of the city's prominent preachers—marshalled the forces of righteousness. So great is the abhorence of legalized gambling that opposition to it united the Baptist and Church of Christ preachers, spiritual guides of groups that usually expend their energies conducting jihads against one another. Armaggedon was at hand; to hear the preachers inveighing against gambling was to learn that godliness and the Christian Way faced potential extermination. A race track in Nashville would provoke a divine retribution that would make Yahweh's punishment of Sodom and Gomorrah mild by comparison. Clerical demagoguery paid off: in August 1987 the children of light beat back the devil's attempt to foist a race track upon Nashville.

The fight then moved to the neighboring county of Williamson, where the sides squared off for round two. Since Williamson's Nashville suburbs are infested with transplanted Yankees, the proposal stood a better chance of approval. The preachers stalked among the country folk, shouting doom and destruction. A local wag suggested a compromise: permit horse racing but require all the horses to be named after books of the Bible. To the dismay of the wicked, the preachers prevailed: Williamson County gamblers will

have to continue to trek to Kentucky or Alabama to indulge
their vice. Or go to Memphis—true to form, the voters of that
city approved a referendum on pari-mutuel betting, thus further plunging themselves, as my Church of Christ preacher
acquaintance would say, into hell.

VII

To the outsider, Southern religion breeds a looniness
found nowhere else in America. In the North, automobile bumpers sport stickers proclaiming the driver's political preferences, favored vacation spots or municipal
patriotism ("I Heart New York"). Southerners more frequently
advertise their religious sentiments: "Trust Jesus," "Honk If
You Love Jesus," "Prepare for Your Finals—Read the Bible,"
"I'm a Fool for Christ—Whose Fool Are You?" Northern van-
dals spray-paint bridges and walls with descriptive four-letter
words that urge various anatomically improbable contor-
tions; their Southern counterparts favor a five-letter word:
"Jesus"—as in "Jesus Is Coming" or "Jesus Is the Answer."
Stark warnings scream from roadside signs: "Repent!" "Hell
Is at Hand!" "The End Is Near!" Technology has added a
new angle to this genre of evangelization. Crudely lettered
wooden signs are harder to find; more often one spots those
portable neon affairs that flash out the gospel. The owner
of a service station near my house uses his sign to promote
godliness, often in tune with the particular season of the year.
On the Fourth of July his sign proclaims: "Without Christ
There Is No Freedom," and for New Year's it reads: "Thanks
to God, Shell and Customers for a Good Year." The Southern
pietist of a more explicitly commercial bent makes good use of
these signs as well, for he can kill two birds with one stone,
as it were: "Jesus Says Ye Must Be Born Again—Area-Size
Rug Sale 20% Off." Christians of a martial inclination find

these signs and bumper stickers a practial way to expound their philosophy: "God, Guts and Guns Made America—Let's Keep All Three." My especial favorite, perhaps because of its subtlety, is: "Kill 'Em All, Let God Sort 'Em Out."

Among Southern writers, Flannery O'Connor best captured the seething fundamentalist imagination. To the non-Southerner, Miss O'Connor's religious grotesques appear to be the product of an especially fertile mind; the Southerner more likely opines that O'Connor simply reported quotidian reality in her short stories. A random reading of Southern newspapers attests to her acute powers of observation. Take, for example, Mrs. Cheryl Prewitt Blackwood of Brentwood, Tennessee. As Miss Cheryl Prewitt of Mississippi she won the crown in the 1980 Miss America contest. At the time, she testified to the miracle that had been wrought in her childhood. An automobile accident had left her with one leg appreciably shorter than the other. In 1974, through the intercession of a faith-healer, she experienced a miracle: her abbreviated limb caught up with the normal one. Mrs. Blackwood capitalized upon her success as a beauty queen by establishing a "Christian Charm School" whose goal was "to train young people in appearance and poise while incorporating Christian ideas for total beauty."

This is mildly O'Connoresque, but not full-throttle O'Connor. For the straight stuff one turns to the saga of Arlene and Luther Gardner, a story O'Connor surely would have entitled "The Precious Freezer." The Gardners live in Estil Springs, Tennessee, southeast of Nashville. In the spring of 1987 they discovered a curious phenomenon: when their neighbor switched on her porch light the bulb cast a shadow onto the upright freezer on the front porch of the Gardners' mobile home. The image was that of the head of Jesus. Pilgrims crowded into the Gardner front yard to stare in awe at what Mrs. Gardner called "my precious freezer." Neighbors grumbled about the traffic congestion and nocturnal hordes, but skeptics were scarce. "I believe in miracles and I believe in Jesus," said a typical witness. "Can't people see this is a warning?" asked Mrs. Gardner.

Pat Robertson and Oral Roberts would probably find it easy to credit the genuineness of this apparition. Robertson, after all, has twice prayed a hurricane off a collision course with Virginia Beach, and Roberts has recently revealed that he has raised the dead. (Well, at least they *looked* dead, he hedges.) These tv preachers, heirs to generations of Elmer-Gantry-like tent revivalists, flourish nowhere so luxuriantly as in the South. The high-tech men of the cloth beam their message nationwide, but the core of their support lies in the South. The Gardners probably tune in regularly to several of these spellbinders.

Southerners harbor an inherited predilection for this form of edification. Since around 1800 the South has been fertile soil for the roving revivalist showman. Technology has created a new form of partnership between revivalist and re-vivalee. Everybody can stay home now—the viewers in Estil Springs, Bucksnort and Bugscuffle (and Atlanta, Nashville, Birmingham and Richmond, one should add, lest city folks surmise that only rubes watch these shows), and Jerry in Lynchburg, Pat in Virginia Beach, Jimmy in Baton Rouge and Oral in Tulsa; alas, Jim and Tammy Faye have departed the environs of Charlotte. The "cool medium" may have drained some of the frenzy from Southern revivalism, but it has not altered the essentials: soul-saving and dollar-collecting remain at the heart of the enterprise.

VIII

The tv preachers have added a new fillip to the old game of stump revivalism. Their message is no longer only the traditional gambit of throw-yourself-upon-Jesus-empty-your-pockets-and-be-saved. The big-name evangelists, cheered and imitated by lesser fry in pulpits across the South, have shouldered the burden of saving America from perdition. A congeries of issues is wrapped up in this herculean task: creationism, school prayer, feminism, homosexual rights, and the granddaddy of them all, secular humanism, a term that often encapsulates all the fears and anxieties of the Southern fundamentalist. These concerns are not uniquely situated in the South; they do, however, flame with a special intensity below the Mason-Dixon line. The tv evangelists pride themselves on their knack for garnering supporters from every nook and cranny of America, but they know, as did the Democratic party of old, that without the Solid South they have little chance of victory. So goes Dixie, so goes the crusade for God and country.

The debate over creationism and evolution is nothing new. It has been around since the late nineteenth century, periodically breaking out in savage warfare just when the rest of the country thought the issue had been put to rest. The current dispute is tame compared to what happened in the 1920s when five Southern states passed laws to curb or prohibit Mr. Darwin's pernicious doctrine. In the most notorious instance the Tennessee legislature proscribed the teaching of evolution in public schools, an act that led to the Scopes trial of 1925. This farcical drama pitted two equally foolish and narrow-minded men—Clarence Darrow and William Jennings Bryan—against one another in a contretempts that degraded both religion and science. But the Southerner's biblical literalism leaves him no choice but to rally to the Bryans of the world, whether in the 1920s or the 1980s. The Bible is either true or false, he reasons, and if you can disprove the veracity of Genesis, then the whole edifice topples.

In rejecting evolution the Southern fundamentalist casts himself as a dim-witted obscurantist who, Northerners assume, also believes that the earth is flat. There is more than a smidgen of truth in this, but on another level one perceives something else. In clinging to a literal Genesis, the Southerner apprehends intuitively that the popularizers of science seek to erect a competing world view to displace the Christian explanation of existence. In the gospel according to scientism, science not only explains all, but can solve all as well. This is nothing but nineteenth-century positivism tricked out in the more fashionable livery of the twentieth century. Though the fundamentalist may be one of Mencken's "gaping primates," he knows something that eluded the Sage of Baltimore: mystery pervades the cosmos, and the truly ignorant man is the one who thinks that science can dispel it. This, not evolution, is the real issue, and though the fundamentalist may be right for the wrong reasons, he is nonetheless right. The world views of scientism and orthodox Christianity cannot be reconciled.

The Southern fundamentalist's visceral grasp of the basic issue lacks the intellectual refinement that would enable him to promote his case effectively. He looks foolish as he peers under beds and rummages through closets to ferret out the secular humanists hiding there. "Secular humanism" is a handy catchword that preachers bandy about to explain the confusion of the modern world. "Darwinism" served the same function in the '20s, and this strategy of oversimplication is no more efficacious now than it was sixty years ago. By his crude analysis of the problem, the fundamentalist dooms himself to ridiculousness, while the truth he champions suffers from his ill-starred defense. He is his own worst enemy.

IX

The Southern Protestant generally believes that America is God's chosen nation, uniquely blessed and divinely appointed to bring enlightenment and the gospel to the benighted races of mankind. This is odd, for this view of America's providential role was brought to these shores by the Puritans of Massachusetts Bay, a people whose descendants bear much responsibility for all that Southerners consider wrong with the world. To a discerning Southerner, the Harvard of 1636 and the Harvard of 1988 are two peas in the same pod. But the Southerner, like the New Englander of old, is a child of the Reformation, and with the ravages of sectional controversy faded to dim memory, he can applaud the Puritans and their vision of a godly commonwealth.

Because of his conflation of Christianity and country, the Southerner is often more strenuously anti-Communist than other Americans. This involves more than a realistic commitment to protecting America's legitimate interests from foreign encroachment. To the Southerner, Communism forms the external counterpart to the internal threat posed by secular humanism. Both threaten America, both are godless, and both would derail the nation from her divine mission. He identifies capitalism—or "free enterprise," as he is wont to say—as the essence of the American Way. In doing so, he sanctifies an economic system and marries Christianity to the dictates of the marketplace. Capitalism especially commends itself to him, for after long years of impoverishment, he has finally managed to squeeze up to the trough where the benefits are dished out. This newfound prosperity only confirms his sense of godliness: Doesn't the Good Lord bless those who keep his commandments?

The right to pray in the public schools is crucial to the Southerner because it is emblematic of the whole idea of a Christian America. Because the South has been Protestant historically, Southerners have been accustomed to a system of public education that supports the dominant ethos. The schools are *public,* but they embody and promote (or at least they *did*) a non-denominational Protestantism. The students are Protestants, the parents and taxpayers are Protestants, the teachers and administrators are Protestants. Who, then, would object to prayer in the schools? Communists and secular humanists, that's who—people dedicated to the destruction of both America and Christianity. The Southern fundamentalist finds it impossible to comprehend that any God-fearing American could want to deprive the South's children of the right to recite a prayer in the classroom. Patriotism and religion are not only compatible and mutually supportive; at bottom, they are one and the same.

Throw in such things as feminism, homosexual rights, abortion and pornography, and one can easily understand the Southern fundamentalist's angry opposition to the tenor of the times. Traditionally the Southerner has believed that politics and religion occupy separate spheres; Southern Baptists, for example, have always ranked among the most watchful guardians of the wall between church and state. But the Southern churchgoer is apt to be more politicized today. He does not look askance when Jerry Falwell preaches politics, nor does he bat an eye when Pat Robertson enters the presidential race. The Southern Bible-believer perceives himself part of a beleaguered minority upon which rests the burden of rescuing America from the pit of destruction. His ancestors identified themselves as a minority resisting the onslaught of abolitionists. More recently, the white Southerner felt put upon by the proponents of racial integration. But sectionalism and race have little to do with the present crisis. The stakes are much higher this time, for they involve nothing less than the fate of Christian truth and the American nation. If this cause is lost, then *all* is lost.

X

This, then, is what our visitor from the North must face if he hopes to settle in the South. To live here is to dwell amongst a people often drunk on old-time religion. Those not part of the culture of fundamentalism can either laugh at it, weep over its misguidedness, or bristle with rage at its arrogance and aggressiveness, but they cannot ignore it: it is ubiquitous. One type of person in particular finds it especially grueling to live with these fundamentalists: the Roman Catholic. For him (if he is a native), the South is both haven and horror, both home and hostile territory. With blacks at last gaining their rightful and full participation in Southern society, the Catholic remains the region's last truly marginal man. He may be the South's sole remaining "nigger," replacing in that role the rising black man, who is, after all, himself most likely a practitioner of the old-time religion.

2. The Pope's Folks in the Land of Cotton

The South is at once the *most* religious and *least* Catholic region of America. Despite the influx of Yankee papists in the past twenty or so years, the South has the smallest percentage of Catholics anywhere in the United States. According to the 1987 edition of *The Official Catholic Directory*, New England, with 41% of its population belonging to the Church, tops all regions. By contrast, the South Atlantic area (Delaware, Maryland, the District of Columbia, Virginia, the Carolinas, Georgia and Florida) is only 8% Catholic. The East South Central region (Kentucky, Tennessee, Alabama and Mississippi) claims an even smaller number: 5%. Only in the West South Central area (Arkansas, Louisiana, Oklahoma and Texas) does the South have a significant concentration of Catholics: 19%.

A breakdown by states further pinpoints the location of Catholics within the region. Maryland is 17% Catholic, and the diocese of Washington, D.C., which includes five of Maryland's counties, is 19%. Significant concentrations also exist in Florida (13%), Kentucky (10%), Texas (20%), and the highest, Louisiana, with 31%. At the other end of the scale, North and South Carolina have Catholic populations that form only 2% of the total in those states. Georgia, Alabama and Arkansas stand at 3%, and Tennessee and Mississippi only slightly higher at 4%. Even within the states that have a fair number of Catholics, they tend to concentrate in certain areas. In Louisiana, for example, the diocese of Houma-Thibedaux in the southern part of the state is 63% Catholic, one of the highest in the entire country; but the diocese of Shreveport in the north is only 5%. In Texas, the diocese of Brownsville is 66% Catholic, while those of Dallas and Fort Worth are only eight and seven percent respectively. Outside a few unique areas, Catholics scarcely dent the South's solid Protestant phalanx.

II

Catholics arrived in what would become the South long before Protestants reached these shores. The sixteenth century belonged to Spain. In 1521 Ponce de Leon, chimera-chaser of the first order, landed on the coast of Florida, only to be driven out by inhospitable Indians. Hernando de Soto followed in 1539, using Florida as a point of departure for a three-year peregrination. He ranged northward to the Blue Ridge Mountains, and then swung back southward all the way to present-day Mobile on the Gulf Coast. He became the first white man to lay eyes upon the Mississippi, a river that would snake its roily waters through the history of the South. He journeyed northward along its course all the way to the present site of Memphis, a fact later commemorated by the city in the naming of one of the bridges that crosses into Arkansas.

Florida formed the focus of the Spanish gambit. They founded St. Augustine in 1565, and from here they launched expeditions into the interior and established missions along the coasts of Georgia and South Carolina. In the 1560s a company of Jesuits settled in the Chesapeake Bay region, only to be wiped out by Indians in 1571. Some of those same Indians were probably still around thirty-six years later to greet the Englishmen who sailed up the James River to plant a Protestant colony.

Gallic avarice soon sniffed the promise of the New World. Spanish venturings evoked a French rejoinder: in 1562 they founded a Huguenot settlement, Port Royal, on the South Carolina coast. The Spaniards refused to tolerate this intrusion, and by the late sixteenth century they had swept the southeastern coast free of rivals. The French were more successful in the interior. As part of their imperial contest with the late-arriving English, they staked title to the Mississippi Valley. Fr. Jacques Marquette, a Jesuit, and Louis Joliet, a trade-hungry compatriot, paddled down the Mississippi in 1673 to the point where the great river swallows the waters of its Arkansas tributary, just above present-day Greenville, Mississippi. A decade later La Salle reached the mouth of the river, claimed the entire region for France, and named it Louisiana in honor of his king. Less than forty years later, the French founded New Orleans, the future queen city of the Deep South.

Later generations of Catholic-hating, xenophobic Southerners would be left to grapple with a piquant irony: the first "Southerners" were Spanish and French; the first "Southern" clergymen, papist priests; the first "Southern" Christians, minions of Rome. But the Southerners of the future were in no danger of facing life with a Catholic religion and Spanish and French forebears. Neither Spain nor France could maintain suzerainty over the region. Though the influence of these people would make a lasting impression along the Gulf Coast and would establish Catholicism as the enduring religion in southern Louisiana, the future lay not with the Catholic powers, but with the English, bitter rivals of France and Spain in both empire-building and religion.

III

It is impossible to untangle the skein of motives that impelled England to enter the imperial contest. The prospects for pecuniary gain and the enhancement of national glory—either singly or in combination—provided sufficient reason for Englishmen to launch the New World experiment. But the religious impulse was always present, even if more subtly in some cases than others. For the Puritans who settled New England, it furnished the primary reason for departing the home shores. They sought refuge from a persecuting Anglican Church that they considered still hopelessly mired in papist superstition and un-Christian practice.

Although religion played a less striking role in the southern colonies, it was not absent from the calculations of the colonizers. By 1607, when three shiploads of Englishmen planted the flag in Virginia, the rent in Christendom had existed for almost a century. Under Queen Elizabeth England had emerged in the late sixteenth century as the most powerful nation in opposition to Rome, a standing confirmed by the defeat of the Spanish Armada in 1588. Imperialism not only augmented England's economic and geopolitical prospects, but it also bolstered the Protestant cause. The passengers who disembarked on the shores of the James River included an Anglican clergyman (a forebear of Pat Robertson) who claimed the land in the name of the God of Protestantism. In a sense, Virginia began its existence as a venture in anti-Catholicism, a Protestant salient projecting into the dark regions already controlled by black-garbed priests of the Romish faith. The Carolinas and Georgia later played a similar part in the continuing struggle between the two divisions of Western Christendom.

Maryland formed the lone exception to the Protestant unanimity of English settlement. George Calvert, Lord Baltimore, sought for his Catholic coreligionists a haven from Protestant hostility at home, and, in confirmation of the mixed motivation of colonizers, the English grandee had an eye for a profitable investment. The Catholic settlers of 1634 were loyal Englishmen, contrary to the aspersions cast upon them. They were no fifth column marching into the heart of English America; they were simply Catholic Englishmen, seeking in their own colony an easier way to be both Catholic and English.

Their Virginia neighbors accepted them as such; the Potomac formed a bridge between two English colonies, not a barrier separating warring religious faiths. The first Marylanders planted the seed of an idea that would come to full flower only in the twentieth century: "American Catholic" was not an oxymoron.

These first Southern Catholics demonstrated something else: they had no desire to persecute Protestants. Cecelius Calvert, who assumed the title Lord Baltimore upon his father's death in 1632, decreed that all Christians should enjoy freedom of religion in the colony. Unlike most men of his era, Calvert believed that Catholics and Protestants could dwell together harmoniously. In 1649 the Maryland assembly reaffirmed this vision in the famous Act of Toleration.

The historian of a cynical bent will quickly point out that these proclamations served the self-interest of Catholics, for from the beginning, they were outnumbered in their own colony. The ships that carried the first settlers to Maryland contained more Protestants than Catholics, and continued migration soon brought floods of non-Catholics. Maryland Catholics had good reason to fear this invasion; their brothers back in England continued to suffer civil and religious disabilities, and, with the exception of Rhode Island and (after 1680) Pennsylvania, the other colonies evidenced little eagerness to grant full equality to Catholics. The decrees did protect Catholics, but they also safeguarded all shades of Protestantism—even Quakers—a tolerance hard to find in other colonies. (Ask the Quakers what kind of welcome they received in Massachusetts Bay Colony.) More important, through these acts, Maryland's Catholics expressed a willingness to live peaceably with fellow colonists not of their faith. Whatever motives undergirded the early documents, they initiated a rare and admirable experiment in Catholic-Protestant relations.

One uses the term "Southern" advisedly in describing these Marylanders, for the concept of the South as a distinct region belongs to the nineteenth century, not to the colonial period. Still, it is fair to assert that Catholics have as good a historical claim to the title "Southerner" as do the most rabid Baptists south of the Mason-Dixon line. The Catholic presence in Maryland waned over the course of the colonial era. They quickly lost political control, and the colony became a Protestant stronghold, albeit one in which Catholic influence survived. In 1692 Catholics suffered the insult of having to abide the establishment of Anglicanism as the colony's official religion. As an added blow, the Calvert family converted to the established church. But the leading families in particular maintained loyalty to the old faith, and from their number came several of the colony's dominant figures in the Revolutionary era of the late eighteenth century.

Among these families, none excelled the Carrolls in contributing distinguished leaders. Charles Carroll, one of the wealthiest men in America, joined the delegates in Philadelphia in signing the Declaration of Independence, the only Catholic to do so. His cousin, Daniel, journeyed to the same city in 1787 with four other Marylanders to represent the state at the Constitutional Convention. When the final document was drawn up, he signed his name to it; only one other Catholic—Thomas Fitzsimmons, a merchant from Philadelphia—shared this distinction. When the new government took office in 1789 Daniel joined the Maryland delegation in the House of Representatives and Charles took one of the state's Senate seats. That Catholicism did not wield great influence in the southern portion of the United States is not surprising; the Church was even less important in the Northern states.

IV

For Southern Catholics the key member of the Carroll clan was Daniel's younger brother, John. Rather than the politics that generally engrossed the Carrolls, John chose a career in the Church. He studied at St. Omer's Seminary in Belgium, entered the Society of Jesus, and returned to Maryland in 1774 on the eve of the break with England. From humble beginnings serving the needs of a scattered flock in Maryland and Virginia, Fr. Carroll rose to leadership of the American Church. He became bishop of Baltimore in 1789, the first resident bishop in the new nation, and in 1808 the pope elevated the see to an archdiocese.

John Carroll laid the foundations of the American Church. He removed any suspicions that Catholicism—frequently identified as a French and Spanish institution—was antagonistic to the principles of the new republic. How "alien" could a Church be whose American leader was a scion of an old Maryland family? The new bishop carefully allayed Protestant fears. When he took the oath of consecration he convinced Rome to delete the words committing him "to seek out and oppose heretics." He avoided polemical confrontations with Protestants, refusing to disturb, as he wrote, "the harmony now subsisting amongst all Christianity in this country. . . ." Most important, Bishop Carroll welcomed the American *modus vivendi* of church-state separation and preached the virtues of religious freedom. He envisioned a democratic Church that would repudiate the monarchical ideal favored by Continental Catholics and the Vatican. In the person of John Carroll Protestants could see that Catholicism accorded with American and republican principles.

Working from a base of only 35,000 Catholics in 1789, Carroll fostered the early growth of the Church. In 1808 he requested more bishops to serve the growing flock, and the Vatican responded by creating new episcopacies in Boston, New York and Philadelphia. A fourth see—one not so familiar to later Catholics—was erected at the same time: Bardstown, Kentucky, in the rapidly growing region beyond the Appalachian Mountains. At the time of the War of 1812 the South possessed two of the first five bishoprics in the new nation, and President Jefferson's recent purchase of the

Louisiana Territory from France had added the Catholics of New Orleans (granted their own bishop in 1815) to the Church's strength in the South. Outside the region, only Pennsylvania boasted a substantial Catholic population.

As further indication of Southern Catholic vitality, the three communities of women religious founded during John Carroll's tenure originated in the South: the Sisters of Charity in Maryland, followed by the Lorettos and the Daughters of Charity of Nazareth in Kentucky. Four more Southern orders would be founded in the antebellum period, one each in Maryland, Kentucky, South Carolina and Louisiana. In addition, twelve European congregations of women religious would labor in the South before the Civil War. The first—and thus far only—American-born saint, Elizabeth Ann Seton, found her vocation in the South. Although a native New Yorker, the widowed Mrs. Seton moved to Maryland in 1808 to escape Protestant animosity in New York City after her conversion, and established a community on a farm near Emmitsburg. In 1813 she became the superior of the Sisters of Charity, the first religious society founded in the United States.

Viewing the country after three decades of nationhood, an observer might reasonably have assumed that Catholicism would thrive more vigorously in the South than in the North. It was, in a sense, a Southern Church, a part of the South as surely as were the Baptist, Methodist, Presbyterian and Episcopal communions.

V

That would not last, and one of the main reasons emerged in the South itself, specifically in the Kentucky to which John Carroll sent one of his new bishops. When Bishop Flaget arrived to assume his duties in 1811 he found himself in a region that had been swept in the previous decade by a series of explosive revivals, part of the Second Great Awakening that wracked the entire country in the early nineteenth century. Until 1800 Episcopalians and Presbyterians dominated the Southern religious scene. The Awakening overwhelmed them and launched the leap to supremacy of Baptists and Methodists, people who would, by the middle of the century, transform the South in their image. Denigrating liturgy, theology and tight structure, they engulfed the South and created the evangelical ethos that still prevails below the Mason-Dixon line.

Bishop Flaget, a Frenchman of culture and refinement, chanted his Latin Mass in a moiling sea of ecstatic Protestant revivalists. While Kentucky's small band of Catholics genuflected, knelt, prayed silently, and breathed the sweet fragrance of incense, their Baptist and Methodist neighbors were boiling with the Spirit in brush-arbor revivals, where believers writhed in the dirt, barked like dogs, moaned in agonies of contrition, wept and shouted. The gulf between Protestantism and Catholicism had seldom been wider or less bridgeable.

Yet even with these differences, Catholics managed to coexist amicably with their Protestant neighbors. Several years before Bishop Flaget's arrival, Fr. Stephen Badin, Kentucky's pioneer priest, reported to Rome that Catholics were suffering from the usual Protestant misunderstanding and ignorance; but, he added, "the non-Catholics who live among the Catholics are less under the influence of prejudice, and they treat us generally as brothers."

More than the rise of Baptists and Methodists widened the gap between Protestants and Catholics. American Catholicism itself experienced a sea change in the nineteenth century. Before then the Church had been small and homogeneous, its constituency not markedly different from that of the Protestant denominations. Its early establishment in Maryland blessed it with a longevity in America equal (and in most cases, superior) to that of the Protestant faiths; Baptists and Methodists were, by comparison, latecomers. Its leading figures—the Carrolls, for example—moved easily and confidently among the social and political elites of the day.

The waves of Irish and Germans that broke upon the shores of the United States from 1820 till the Civil War altered the Church irrevocably. It not only grew immensely in numbers, but its power and influence—the sheer magnitude of its presence—swelled apace. Northern cities began to burst with Catholics, a people who were . . . well, *different*. The Germans and Irish bristled with clannishness; the former clung to their native language, while the Irish spoke an English barely intelligible to old-stock Americans. Moreover, the Irish occupied the lowest rung on the social ladder; they were, in the eyes of Americans of an earlier arrival, abysmally poor, coarse and crude, and their hovels and shanties teemed with hordes of ragged children. And they were papists.

By 1860 the Catholic Church barely resembled the institution of 1820. It was now the foreign body that it had not been at the nation's founding. Oddly enough, Southerners, now predominantly Baptist and Methodist, revealed less immediate aversion to Catholicism than did Northerners. This arose from no especial enlightenment on the part of Southerners, but from the fact that most of the newcomers settled in the North. Immigrants sought jobs and opportunity for advancement; the South, dominated by an agrarian slave economy, offered little of either. The North absorbed the Germans and Irish, and their presence brought the social dislocation, friction, misunderstanding and painful adjustment that inevitably follow in the train of massive immigration.

Some of the new arrivals struck out southward, but these adventuresome souls settled mainly in the region's seaboard and river cities, where the rural focus of slavery necessitated a complement to the available work force. The initial settlement of Irish Catholics in Nashville, Tennessee, came in 1819 when a construction company hired a crew of bridge-builders to erect a span across the Cumberland River. Thirty men arrived from Pittsburgh with their families, built the bridge, settled down and established the Irish community in Nashville. On occasion, planters would hire gangs of Irishmen for jobs too dangerous to risk valuable slaves. Those who survived the rigors of such toil often remained to become Southerners. The greatest spur to the growth of Irish Catholic communities in the South came from the arrival of the railroads and the laborers that built them. Thomas Stritch, historian of the Nashville diocese, notes that "there is scarcely a Catholic center in Tennessee not made or confirmed by the railroads."

By the eve of the Civil War, Richmond, Norfolk, Charleston, Louisville, Nashville, Memphis, New Orleans and Mobile all boasted entrenched Catholic populations. To take only one example, by 1860 Richmond's Catholics made up one-quarter of that city's population. Many of these cities still bear the imprint of this settlement in areas known to old-timers as "Germantown" or "Irish Hill." The South's oldest Catholic churches generally date their founding to the decade or so before the Civil War.

The South easily absorbed these numbers; they neither altered the Baptist-Methodist ethos, nor exercised appreciable influence upon the Southern way of life. But even though Southerners did not feel threatened by the Catholic presence, they tended to perceive the Church—once firmly a part of the South—as an alien institution. Its strength in the North lent to Catholicism an identity with a region and culture to which Southerners displayed mounting aversion. The North, they lamented, vomited up every variety of weirdness: Transcendentalists, Unitarians, utopian socialists, abolitionists, health reformers, free-love advocates, feminists—and Roman Catholics.

Despite the shift of the Church's center from the South to the North, Southern Catholics continued to play a role in both the life of the American Church and in the society and politics of the South. Throughout the antebellum period Baltimore maintained primacy as the chief city of American Catholicism, its archbishop serving as titular head of the Church in the United States. Maryland, Kentucky and Louisiana remained loci of Catholic strength and influence. One of the brightest stars of the hierarchy was John England, the Irish-born bishop of Charleston from the creation of the see in 1820 until his death in 1842. During his two-decade tenure England was perhaps the most influential Catholic churchman in the United States. Among other accomplishments, he founded the first Catholic newspaper in the country, the *United States Catholic Miscellany*. When he died, not only did Catholics rue their loss, but all Charleston mourned.

Catholics also exercised authority in the secular realm. William Gaston represented North Carolina in the House of Representatives during the War of 1812 and later rose to the chief justiceship of the North Carolina supreme court. Richard Brent, John Carroll's nephew, served Virginia in both the House of Representatives and the U.S. Senate, and Anthony M. Keiley was one of the state's most influential newspaper editors in the antebellum period. John B. Floyd was governor of Virginia from 1849–1852, the second Virginia governor of that name—his father, also a Catholic, held the position in the 1830s. In the 1850s he assumed leadership of the Democratic party in the state, and in 1857 President James Buchanan selected him for the post of Secretary of War. The most significant Catholic in the antebellum South was Roger Brooke Taney, scion of two of Maryland's oldest Catholic families. In 1831 President Jackson appointed him Attorney General, and when John Marshall died in 1835, Taney won confirmation as Chief Justice of the United States, a seat he would not relinquish until his death thirty years later.

VI

But these men were exceptions that proved the rule. By the time of the Civil War, a once strongly *Southern* Catholic Church had been transformed into a largely Northern institution. A caveat is called for: it would be a gross mistake to suggest that the war was in any sense a conflict between a Protestant South and a Catholic North. Millions of Catholics poured into the Northern states in the decades before 1860, but the North remained predominantly Protestant. The Civil War involved a host of friction points, but religion was not one of them. Although German and Irish Catholics formed a substantial element in the Union armies that ravaged the Confederacy, one doubts that Southerners took much cognizance of the religious affiliation of the invaders; a Yankee was a Yankee, and it was the blue uniform that mattered, not the fact that its wearer might have a crucifix strung round his neck or a rosary in his haversack.

Something else obviated hostility toward Catholicism as the religion of many of the invaders: the Confederate armies contained their own contingent of Catholics. Soldiers from New Orleans and the lower parishes of Louisiana were Catholics, and though neither Maryland nor Kentucky seceded, many of their Catholic sons fought for the South. The Germans and Irish who had settled in the South's cities also enlisted in the Confederate armies. In Knoxville, Tennessee, for example, the city's Irish Catholics sided solidly with the Confederacy, an unusual stance in East Tennessee, a region almost completely Unionist in sentiment. Protestant rebels had no reason to question the loyalty and dedication of their Catholic compatriots.

The Catholic hierarchy in the South did not discourage sectional loyalty; one could be both a Confederate and a good Catholic. Bishop John Quinlan of Mobile probably voiced the sentiments of most Southern churchmen when he announced his support for the cause: "While regretting the dismemberment of this great republic—and heavens knows we would do all we could legitimately to preserve it—we would not purchase union at the expense of justice."

Catholics have at times been accused of holding a dual allegiance that prevents them from being fully American. John F. Kennedy felt the sting of this nasty slur in 1960, and part of his

campaign strategy entailed an effort to convince Protestants—
especially Southern Democratic ones—that, forced to choose
between pope and Constitution, he would opt for the latter.
This charge of dual allegiance did not surface in the South
during its quest for independence.

In *Gone With the Wind,* that most *Southern* of Southern novels, Margaret Mitchell (herself raised a Catholic) created the archetypal Southern family of popular imagination,
the O'Haras. As the name suggests, the O'Haras are Irish
Catholics, and if Gerald wears his Catholicism lightly, his
wife is devout. Scarlett, the quintessential Southern belle and
heroine, is, *mirabile dictu!,* the product of a Catholic upbringing, though as everyone knows, Miss Scarlett has more important things on her mind than Masses and missals.

In *The Fathers,* a novel published in 1938, two years after
Gone With the Wind, Allen Tate created his own Catholic
Southerner as protagonist. George Posey is descended from
a distinguished Maryland family, and when he marries a
daughter of the Virginia gentry, none of his wife's people
questions his religion. Posey is a Southerner and an aristo-
crat; that he is a Catholic makes no difference. Although he
is not a uniformly admirable character, his flaws stem not
from his religion, but from his failure to embody fully the
eighteenth-century virtues of his elderly father-in-law, Major
Buchan. When the crisis of secession bursts upon Virginia,
Posey smuggles arms for the nascent rebels, and during the
war he serves the cause heroically. In this he is typical of
many flesh-and-blood Maryland Catholics. Sargent Shriver,
a notable figure in the Kennedy years, springs from one of
Maryland's historic Catholic families; one of his forebears was
a general in the Army of Northern Virginia.

A number of Catholics figured prominently in the Confederate cause. Two former Marylanders—Raphael Semmes and
James Ryder Randall—both won enduring fame from the conflict. Semmes, a graduate of the Naval Academy, moved to
Alabama in the 1840s; when the war broke out he entered

the Confederate navy and eventually attained the rank of admiral. Randall settled in New Orleans in his youth; here he wrote "Maryland, My Maryland," an angry, defiant composition that Lee's army used as a marching song until the bitter defeat at Antietam Creek in September 1862. (Despite the efforts of neo-abolitionists to substitute a new state song, "Maryland, My Maryland" remains official.) The most important Catholic army officer was General P. G. T. Beauregard of Louisiana, but other Catholics rose to high rank—General William Hardee of Georgia, for one. Perhaps the most prominent Catholic civilian official was Stephen Mallory, a native of Florida, who served as Jefferson Davis's secretary of the navy.

The Catholic priest was not an unfamiliar figure in the Confederate cause; fifteen of them were chaplains in the Southern armies, while others served without formal appointment. When the war started, Fr. Hippolyte Gache, a French Jesuit, was teaching at Spring Hill College near Mobile. He entered Confederate service as a chaplain to minister to the Catholics under the colors. He accompanied Lee's troops in a number of campaigns, and in a letter to a fellow priest back in Alabama, Fr. Gache remarked that the General was "very favorable toward Catholics and he has the greatest esteem for them." In the same letter he asserted: "You see then, our highest officers are not ill-disposed toward Catholicism." Fr. Gache spent part of the war in Lynchburg, Virginia, a city that provided a hospital center for wounded Confederate soldiers. When a smallpox epidemic broke out in the wards, the Protestant clergymen refused to go near the dying, for fear of contracting the disease. Fr. Gache remained at his post, not only to minister to dying Catholics, but to succor and comfort Protestant soldiers. He survived the epidemic and the war to return to Spring Hill to resume the task of educating Southern Catholics.

Fr. John Bannon came to the United States from his native Ireland in 1853. At the war's outset he was pastoring in

St. Louis, a city of divided loyalties. Fr. Bannon sided with the South, and signed on as chaplain in the army of General Sterling Price of Missouri. In 1863 he was appointed Confederate commissioner to Ireland, a position he used to promote the cause in his native land. In 1864 he accompanied Bishop Patrick Lynch of Charleston to Rome in a fruitless effort to win the Vatican's diplomatic recognition of the Confederate States of America.

Fr. Emmeran Bliemel, a native of Bavaria, was not as fortunate as Gache and Bannon. When Union troops seized his church in Nashville and converted it into a hospital, he joined the 10th Tennessee Regiment, a unit of Irish Catholics from Nashville, as its chaplain. He used the cover of his clerical collar to move in and out of the city, each time smuggling out precious medical supplies and other contraband. Fr. Bliemel was killed near Atlanta in August 1864 while administering the last rites to a slain soldier. In 1983 the Sons of Confederate Veterans belatedly commemorated his bravery with the Confederate Medal of Honor.

Less well known is the war work of Catholic sisters. Wherever hospitals were filled with wounded and sick soldiers, there the sisters were, augmenting the secular nursing corps. The impact of these women cannot be measured, but one suspects that many a suffering Southern boy met his first Catholic in the person of a nun, who consoled him with a kind word and gentle hand. These women are the most truly unsung heroines of the war.

Catholic priests adamantly supported the war on the home front. Fr. Thomas Becker, a native of Pittsburgh, graduate of the University of Virginia and a convert, was appointed to a parish in Martinsburg, Virginia, in 1860. This part of Virginia was rife with Unionist sentiment, an anti-secessionism that would lead Martinsburg to join the new state of West Virginia in 1863. Fr. Becker, an ardent secessionist, refused to bow to prevailing sentiment, a refusal that induced him to ignore a government order calling for clergymen to offer public prayers in support of the Union. He was arrested and jailed briefly for his recalcitrance. A similar fate befell Fr. William Elder, the bishop of Natchez, Mississippi. Ordered by occupying troops to pray for President Lincoln, the bishop refused. His obduracy won him the honor of arrest.

The South bestowed the title "Poet of the Confederacy" upon a Catholic priest, the famous (at least in the South) Fr. Abram Ryan, a native of Maryland, who spent the war years in Tennessee. His poems—especially "The Conquered Banner" and "The Sword of Robert E. Lee"—won him the enduring devotion of generations of Southerners, who turned to poetry to assuage the pain of defeat. His collected poems, published in 1879, went through forty printings in the next thirty years. Thomas Stritch says of Ryan: "He was, in the South, what Bishop Fulton Sheen was to the country during the days of his television fame."

Southern Catholics supported the Confederate cause, gave their lives in the abortive quest for independence, and suffered the crippling consequences of defeat. Their efforts won the admiration of their compatriots, and it was the unusual Protestant who in 1865 could espy any reason to question the Southernness of Catholics who lived in Dixie. Significantly, the Ku Klux Klan, founded in 1866 to defend the principles for which the South had fought, never mentioned Catholics as among those who had betrayed the cause. Rumor has it that some of the Klan's founders were Catholics. In its second incarnation in the 1920s the Klan would make anti-Catholicism a prime recruiting pitch; that the Catholic Church somehow subverted the Southern creed never crossed the minds of those who rode with the first Klan.

VII

In the 1880s America witnessed the beginnings of a fresh wave of immigration, one that would eventually surpass in numbers the Germans and Irish of the antebellum period. The migrants came this time mostly from Southern and Eastern Europe (though the Irish and Germans continued to arrive in reduced numbers), and millions of them were Catholics, especially from Poland and Italy. Just as before the Civil War, these people bypassed the South. They settled in large cities—Boston, New York, Philadelphia, Buffalo, Cleveland, Chicago, Milwaukee—where they could cluster with their countrymen and find work. Baltimore was the only Southern city (and that in a border state) that absorbed large numbers of them, although many Italians settled in New Orleans. The coal fields of western Virginia and eastern Kentucky drew some Catholic immigrants, but not enough to make a critical difference. The South did not possess the large cities and heavy industry to attract these newcomers, and in the cities it did have, Negroes furnished the cheap, unskilled labor that often provided immigrants with their first job. In addition, the South, once a prosperous land, had entered upon a long night of bleak poverty, a pall of indigence that would not be dispelled until World War Two and after. Immigrants—whether Catholic or not—had little reason to seek their fresh start in the South.

Few prominent Catholics emerged in the postwar South to make their mark. Catholics were even less visible in the late nineteenth century than in the antebellum era. Charles Gayarré, a Louisianan, was the South's most distinguished historian in the immediate postwar years, having won fame in the 1840s and 1850s by chronicling the history and literature of his native state. But Gayarré's stature as a writer was overshadowed by his fellow Louisianan, George Washington Cable, a Presbyterian.

Thomas Price was born in North Carolina on the eve of the Civil War. Ordained to the priesthood, he spent the 1880s and 1890s in a herculean but bootless labor to convert his fellow North Carolinians. Fr. Price's best-known feat occurred outside his native state: in 1911 he joined another priest to found the Maryknoll order. Ironically, the Maryknolls, with their penchant for Third World revolutionaries, would later become the *bête-noire* of commie-hating Southern patriots, who little knew that one of their compatriots had established the order.

The most famous Catholic in the postbellum South was James Gibbons, born in Baltimore in 1834 of Irish immigrant parents. He was named bishop of Richmond in 1873, and during his tenure he published *The Faith of Our Fathers*, a book that brought him nationwide attention. The Catholic historian John J. Delaney has called this volume "probably the best-selling Catholic book in the history of the Church in the United States." In 1877 Gibbons assumed command of the archdiocese of Baltimore, a position he held for the next forty-four years. As Archbishop of Baltimore he maintained the see's primacy in the American Church, and as Cardinal (after 1886) he won recognition as the leader of the Church in this country. Not till his death in 1921 did Maryland fully surrender her position as the focal point of American Catholicism. By then, however, the Catholic Church had long since forfeited its Southern credentials.

VIII

The South that entered the twentieth century claimed relatively few Catholics within its borders. Maryland boasted a larger Catholic population than ever, owing to the recent arrival of immigrants in Baltimore, but then, Maryland was rapidly losing its Southern character. Southern Louisiana and New Orleans remained solidly Catholic, and central Kentucky and the city of Louisville continued to evidence a strong Catholic flavor. Beyond that, the South possessed no large concentrations of Catholics. River and seaboard cities still contained communities of Irish and Germans, and throughout the region one could find scatterings of Rome's followers.

They were thoroughly Southern, and their Protestant neighbors generally accepted them as such. Southern Protestants evinced the normal range of ignorance, misconception and suspicion about the Roman Catholic Church, but no deeply rooted anti-Catholicism marred Protestant-Catholic relations in the South. That would change in the new century.

3. Catholic-Baiting with a Southern Accent

Catholic Southerners suffered a rude shock early in the twentieth century: they discovered that their neighbors did not much like Catholics. This is not to suggest that till then the South had been unsullied by anti-Catholicism. It had existed from the start. Save for Maryland, the Southern colonies were offspring of the Reformation; they were—even if only indirectly—a means to advance the fortunes of Protestantism. Throughout most of the colonial era Catholicism, in the form of France and Spain and their New World dependencies, loomed as a threat to the transplanted Englishmen of North America. The Southern colonists feared the Spanish especially, for they controlled the lands that bordered the southern frontier. The American Revolution stood the old dichotomy of virtuous Protestants versus wicked Catholics on its head, for Americans secured their independence only with the aid of their former papist nemeses, Spain and, especially, France. Acquisition of Louisiana from France in 1803 and then Florida from Spain in 1819 removed the last occasion for mutterings about Jesuit plots being hatched along the South's borders.

Distaste for Catholics found a new focus in the nineteenth century: the German and Irish immigrants who streamed into the young nation. Because the South did not have to absorb many of these newcomers, it did not seethe with the

Romanophobia that agitated the North from the late 1820s onward. Northeastern cities reeled from the shock of incorporating hordes of the recent arrivals, and native Protestants in these areas retaliated against the importunate strangers. Animosity escalated to violence in the 1830s. Protestant thugs destroyed St. Mary's church in New York City in 1831, and three years later a mob torched a convent in Charlestown, Massachusetts. A decade after this, Philadelphia, belying the Greek meaning of its name, witnessed a three-day rampage that leveled a seminary, two churches and scores of Catholic dwellings.

The nativist anger of the '30s found political expression in the early 1840s, as anti-immigrant sentiment crystallized in efforts to restrict the voting and officeholding rights of the newly arrived. The reaction reached its height in New York City, where Protestant anxiety was exacerbated by the city's aggressive Catholic bishop, John Hughes, who demanded that the state contribute tax monies to support parochial schools. He further incensed Protestants by insisting that Catholic, children in public schools be excused from reading the King James Version of the Bible. In response, nativists elected one of their own to the mayor's office in 1844.

The South did not go untouched by this anxiety. The region did not have to grapple with the myriad problems—psychological, social, political and economic—engendered by the arrival of masses of immigrants, most of whom settled outside the boundaries of the South. But by the late 1830s Southerners had launched that long season of defensiveness and acute sensitivity to perceived threats that would culminate in the rending of the Union. A raft of issues and events fed this burgeoning anxiety, but at its heart lay Southern fears over challenges to the institution of slavery. In their scrutiny of every conceivable source of anti-slavery agitation, Southerners inevitably posed the question: Did the Catholic Church constitute a threat to the Southern system of forced labor and race control? After all, by the 1830s Southerners found it easy to lump the Church with other Yankee institutions and ideas that sought to disturb the equanimity of Southern society.

Pope Gregory XVI furnished Southerners with the evidence they needed to indict the Catholic Church for meddling. In 1839 he issued an encyclical condemning the African slave trade. The United States had outlawed this commerce in human flesh thirty years earlier, but that did not mitigate Southerners' anger with the Vatican. In their raw sensitivity, they interpreted criticism of any aspect of the "peculiar institution" as tantamount to abolitionism. Bishop John England of Charleston, South Carolina, a city that contained the most exposed nerves in all the South, bore the brunt of Southern apologists' ire. They assailed him as an abolitionist, and the more unsavory elements of the city's populace muttered threats against the cathedral and England himself. That England had opened a school for free blacks aggravated the situation. The bishop hastened to calm the wrath of his fellow Charlestonians. He closed the school and reassured his critics that he was no William Lloyd Garrison. He defended the pope's statement, but he also exonerated the Vatican from the charge of condemning the institution of slavery as it existed in the South. England's placation succeeded, and the agitation receded, but suspicion of the Church did not disappear.

The American or Know-Nothing party arose in the early 1850s to capitalize on continuing Protestant restiveness. (The party's name came from the answer that members, sworn to secrecy, gave when queried about the organization: "I don't know.") For a brief spell it flourished in the turbulent political waters of the decade before the Civil War.

Know-Nothingism reached its peak outside the South, but—given Southerners' hypersensitivity by the 1850s— enough tinder existed in the South to light the fires there, too. Maryland, despite its Catholic heritage, succumbed briefly to the fever. In 1854 the Know-Nothings elected their candidate as mayor of Baltimore. A year later the party captured control of the state legislature, and in 1856 Maryland was the lone state won by Millard Fillmore, the Know-Nothing presidential candidate. A Tennessean stood as the Know-Nothings' vice-presidential nominee in 1856, and within his state, the city of Knoxville, home to a fair number of Irishmen, fostered a wave of Catholic-hating. Little violence occurred here, but in 1855, with the city's new church under construction, Catholics did feel compelled to ring the site with armed guards. In Virginia the Know-Nothings mounted a campaign to win the governor's office. Bishop McGill of Richmond furnished a focal point for anti-Catholic sentiment. Fears of divided Catholic loyalties fueled the animosity toward the bishop and his flock. What would Catholics do, the Know-Nothings queried, if the pope were to invade Virginia? The leap from the ridiculous to the horrific occurred in Louisville, Kentucky: on a day in 1855 known as "Bloody Monday," mobs stormed the city's Catholic neighborhoods, leaving in their wake the murdered bodies of almost one hundred Catholics.

Despite such an appalling event, the fact remains that Know-Nothingism did not transform the South into a cauldron of hatred against Catholics and immigrants. To begin with, there simply were not enough of either to fuel the fantasies of even the most paranoid defenders of Southern institutions. The real issue for Southerners arose from the growing tension over North-South sectionalism, and the Catholic Church, despite its increasingly Northern cast, was largely irrelevant to that issue.

More important, the Church in the South, as well as individual Catholics there, largely shared the Protestant Southerner's urge to defend the South against Yankee aspersions. Catholics were as much Southerners as they were Catholics, and as North-South animosities mounted, the former identity tended to supersede the latter. As Randall M. Miller, a historian of antebellum Southern Catholicism, avers: "The Church won social and political acceptance in the South by sanctifying the secular order of slavery and states' rights." Beyond this, by mid-century Southern Catholics appeared more akin to their Protestant neighbors than ever, for they had embraced two things dear to the hearts of Baptists and Methodists: the crusade against alcohol and a Catholic version of revivalism in the form of the parish mission conducted by peripatetic priests. Taken together, these facets of Southern Catholicism cut the ground from under agitators bent on arousing hatred against the Catholic Church. Much to the relief of Southern Protestants, they saw that Catholics, too, could be captives of culture. Catholic enthusiasm for the war against Yankee aggression sealed the image of the Catholic as loyal Southerner.

One other event from the antebellum period bears mention. The war with Mexico in 1846–1848 induced a sprinkling of Catholic-hating in parts of the South. Texas, the root cause of the war, had been settled largely by Tennesseans, Louisianans, Alabamians and Mississippians, and the kinfolk who did not join the exodus reacted with fury as reports of Mexican atrocities filtered back home. Mexicans were Catholics, Texans Protestants, and it was tempting to frame the conflict in religious terms. Rather than hatred, however, the crisis more often evoked contempt for the decadence and decrepitude of Catholic Mexico. The easy defeat of the Mexicans confirmed the imperial destiny of Protestant America, and demonstrated that God would not permit a backward papist nation to impede America's manifest destiny. Whatever enmity the war excited against Catholics was soon swallowed up by the greater antagonism toward Yankees.

II

Not until the early twentieth century did anti-Catholicism enjoy a sustained vitality in the South. From the least anti-Catholic region of America in the nineteenth century, it metamorphosed into the locus of the most poisonous strain of anti-Catholicism the United States has ever seen. This did not stem from an increase in the number of Catholics, for they remained, as they had always been, a minuscule segment of the population. Why, then, did the *least* Catholic part of the country become the *most* anti-Catholic?

One arrives at an answer, not by looking for direct causes, but by searching out events and ideas that contributed obliquely to the phenomenon. The Spanish-American War of 1898 furnishes a good place to start. This *opéra-bouffe* skirmish encouraged Southerners to reaffirm their Americanism. Since the Civil War the Southerner had labored under suspicions of un-Americanism; he had, as demagogic Northern politicians were quick to remind, nearly destroyed God's chosen nation. The war against Spain enabled the Southerner to redeem himself once and for all by fighting for the Stars and Stripes. The sons and grandsons of Union and Confederate veterans sealed their solidarity at the expense of Spain, an old antagonist and still as Catholic as ever.

Spain's declining imperial fortunes confirmed—as had the war with Mexico—the decadence and weariness of the Catholic religion. Protestantism energized hardy Anglo-Saxons to stride across continents and span oceans; Catholicism belonged to an antiquated and unenlightened past. The painless victory ("a splendid little war," John Hay called it) cast the religion of Spain in a contemptible light. To pragmatic American Protestants, if a religion didn't work (that is, bring success), it was no good.

The war did not, however, stimulate any particularly harsh sentiments toward Southern Catholics. Their patriotism was unimpeachable; they evinced no sympathy for Catholic Spain. If anything, Catholics hastened to dissociate themselves from the idea of trans-Atlantic solidarity with their coreligionists. In a widely circulated sermon, Bishop Thomas Byrne of Nashville reaffirmed Catholic patriotism. "We are true Americans," he proclaimed. "And we are loyal to our country and to its flag, and obedient to the highest degree to the supreme authority of our nation." Still, those malignant Spaniards were *Catholics,* and even if Southern Catholics were blameless, their Church was, in some sense, on the wrong side of the conflict.

The Spanish War coincided with the white South's attempt to establish a new mode of race control. Between 1890 and 1910 individual Southern states erected the Jim Crow system that would regulate race relations for the next half-century. What possible connection could this have with anti-Catholicism? No direct one—that is certain. But there does appear to be an indirect and subtle one.

The white South had arrived at the segregationist conclusion only after years of uncertainty, indecision and turmoil. As the historian C. Vann Woodward has argued in *The Strange Career of Jim Crow* (1954), the South did not institute thoroughgoing separatism as soon as it threw off the yoke of Reconstruction. Not until about 1890 did the movement begin in earnest, and not until the eve of World War One did Jim Crow emerge in full panoply. The role of blacks in Southern society became embroiled in the savage political controversy of the 1880s and 1890s, a conflict that pitted agrarian have-nots—the Populists—against the cities and their political, legal and business elites. In the ensuing struggle both sides manipulated the black vote to gain the upper hand. Ultimately the fear of racial equality convinced warring whites that blacks must be expelled altogether from politics and consigned to a separate and constricted sphere. State legislatures implemented this decision in the two decades after 1890.

How does Catholicism figure in? Having established segregation, white Southerners had to preserve unanimity at home and defend their *modus vivendi* from external threats. With scarcely a dissenting voice, Protestant clergymen lent their assent and often active support to Jim Crowism. Should a preacher break ranks he could be disciplined by his church members under the congregational polity that dominated Southern church life. Even in churches that belonged to hierarchical denominations—notably Episcopal and Methodist—individual congregations wielded often decisive influence. Religion lay at the heart of the white Southerner's world; it was crucial that his church support his social arrangements.

Protestants asked: What of the Catholics who took their marching orders from a priest beholden ultimately to the pope in Rome? Although Southern Catholics evidenced no especial disagreement with segregation, their loyalty to a foreign potentate rendered them suspect. Moreover, the Catholic was, in often indefinable ways, *different* from other Southerners. He worshiped differently; he likely bore a German, Irish or French surname; he probably lived in a city instead of in the salubrious and God-fearing countryside; and most of his coreligionists dwelt in a North that at times grumbled threateningly over the injustice of blatant racial inequality in the South (but not in the North). The Southern Catholic did not seem fully bound by the manners and mores that governed the South. If not a fifth columnist, the Catholic was at least a *tertium quid* who belonged neither to the white Protestant South, nor to the equally Protestant black South.

III

Two intellectual currents of the late nineteenth century fostered anti-Catholicism. The first arose from the South's opposition to Darwinism and the general idea of biological evolution. The South was (and remains) the most adamantly anti-evolutionist region of the country. The reason is not hard to discern, and it has more to do with religion than with science. To the typical Southern Protestant there was simply no way to square Darwinism with a literal reading of *Genesis*. The Southerner took his Bible, like his whiskey, neat; that God had created the earth, the heavens and all living things in six days could not be denied, save by those eager to traduce God, Holy Writ and the Christian religion. Opposition to

Darwinism mounted slowly in the late nineteenth-century South, mainly because so few Southerners espoused the theory that the faithful did not feel threatened. But as scientific and popular sentiment in favor of evolution grew, Southerners raised the alarm.

The anti-Catholic angle was oblique, but no less significant for that. Anti-evolutionists tended to indict the Catholic Church for being soft on Darwinism. This arose not from positive statements of the Church or individual Catholics, but from the failure of Catholics to leap to the attack on Darwinism. To many Protestants, this indicated covert acceptance of the philosophy. This did not surprise Southern Protestants; after all, everyone knew that Catholics played fast and loose with divine writ. The Church—according to popular wisdom—prohibited the laity from reading the Bible; how else keep those benighted Catholics in thrall to such an unscriptural institution as the papacy? The Catholic appeal to tradition and papal authority only confirmed the charge that Catholics did not consider the Bible the sole authoritative guide to Christian belief. A Catholic was worse than an atheist in the eyes of Bible-believing Southerners: the latter openly announced his enmity to the faith, but the former masqueraded as a Christian while boring away at the foundations of the faith.

The second idea that inflamed hostility toward Catholicism was premillennialism. Most Catholics have either never heard of this teaching or, if they have stumbled upon it, it strikes them as another example of Protestant wackiness. Premillennialism is not so easily dismissed in Protestant circles, especially among the fundamentalists who dominate the South. There are more varieties of premillennialism than breeds of coon hound, but certain aspects of the doctrine circulate broadly. In its simplest form it contends that we are dwelling in the last days of this groaning creation. Christ will come again suddenly and soon to destroy the wicked and reward the righteous. Proof for this apocalypticism comes from the prophetic utterances in the Bible, especially in *Daniel* and *Revelation*. Much in these two books perplexes those who do not hold the key to unlock the cryptic meaning. Premillennialists claim to possess that key: turn the lock, open the door, and all is revealed. By deciphering the coded passages, by discerning the portents of imminent destruction, and by calculating time sequences (*Daniel*'s 2300 days, for example), premillennialists purport not only to know that the end is near, but, in the case of a few hardy souls, to know approximately when the curtain will drop.

Premillennialism first rose to prominence in the United States when William Miller, a Baptist preacher from upstate New York, predicted that the Second Coming would occur in 1843. When the year passed with no divine visitation, Miller, admitting a miscalculation, reset the date for October 1844. The Millerites, as his followers were known, were devastated when their prophet failed them again. Though they lost faith in Miller's computational skills, they did not surrender their belief in the nearness of the Second Advent. Regrouping in the face of disappointment and the mockery of the heathen, they formed the Seventh-Day Adventist denomination and several smaller sects.

The Millerite movement did not touch the antebellum South, but a later version of premillennialism did catch on. Brought to America after the Civil War by followers of the Englishman John Nelson Darby, dispensationalism soon won devotees in the South, especially among Baptists and the emerging pentecostal sects. Why the South proved receptive to this wave of millennial teaching is hard to determine. The tenor of the times probably had something to do with it. In the 1840s anything that emanated from above the Mason-Dixon line was suspect in the South; by the early twentieth century this was less true. If anyone had reason to embrace apocalypticism it was surely Southerners, who had seen their homeland ravaged by Mr. Lincoln's version of an apocalyptic devastation. Perhaps the Southern mind provided fertile soil in which to cultivate the idea of the fragility of man's creations. For whatever reason, premillennialism, usually of the dispensational strain, spread rapidly among Southern fundamentalists as the twentieth century advanced. Today it is widespread in Baptist groups and among pentecostals. Jerry Falwell, Pat Robertson and Jimmy Swaggart are its most visible and articulate promoters.

Premillennialism nurtures anti-Catholicism because it interprets certain symbols in *Daniel* and *Revelation* as references to the papacy and the Catholic Church. The "three-horned beast" of *Revelation* is generally taken to be the papacy, and John the Revelator's allusions to the "Whore of Babylon" apply to the Catholic Church. For many premillennialists, the pope is the Anti-Christ who seeks to usurp Christ's primacy and to seduce believers down the road to perdition. The premillennial rendering of prophecy identifies the Catholic Church as a pagan institution that hopes to snuff out the candle of biblical truth and shroud the world in darkness. Catholicism is not simply a misguided version of Christianity; it is the weapon with which Satan intends to destroy the faithful remnant. Scratch a premillennialist, and one likely finds a Catholic-baiter. Jimmy Swaggart is simply more candid than his more refined colleagues.

IV

Although these varieties of anti-Catholicism heated up in the late nineteenth century, one thing was missing: a charismatic leader who could evoke the deepest fears and antipathies, and forge them into a concentrated assault on the Catholic Church. Thomas E. Watson was made to order. Born in rural Georgia in 1856, Watson reached manhood in the bleakest era of the South's history. Quick-witted, energetic and idealistic, he yearned to alleviate the misery and privation that gripped the farms and small towns of the state. In the 1880s he joined the rebellion of Georgia farmers against the lawyers, corporate executives and politicians who pulled the state's economic and political strings from their plush offices in Atlanta. By the 1890s he emerged as not only the leader of Georgia's Populists, but as a key player in the agrarian revolt that engulfed much of the South and the Great Plains.

Watson blatantly advocated class conflict—the have-nots against the haves—and in his efforts to unite the former he bridged the racial divide, urging small farmers of both races to combine against their common oppressors. The tumult generated by Watson's temerity crystallized the movement to exclude blacks from Southern politics, a policy that Watson himself—weary of his opponents' cynical manipulation of the black vote—eventually approved.

Until the turn of the century Watson concentrated his fury on economic disparity, but in the years before World War One he began lashing out at different foes. Disheartened by repeated failures, embittered toward the Populists who had ditched him to support the Democrat William Jennings Bryan in 1896, and frustrated by his futile attempt to overcome the white Southerner's obsession with skin pigmentation, he turned to demagoguery. Chimeras skittered through his brain: plots, cabals, conspiracies and hidden machinations lurked everywhere. He reviled blacks whose support he had once solicited; he welcomed their disfranchisement and lauded the practice of lynching as a check on criminality. The intrigues of international Jewry fevered his brain with grotesque images, prompting him to add anti-Semitism to his arsenal of hatreds. The Leo Frank case—the wrongful conviction of a Georgia Jew for the murder of a factory girl—elicited every ounce of Watson's venom. Frank's murder at the hands of a lynch mob in the summer of 1915 owed much to Watson's campaign against the "lascivious pervert."

Catholicism furnished his next target. In the 1910s he excoriated the Catholic Church so relentlessly that, as his biogra-

pher Vann Woodward remarks: "Tom Watson became almost
as closely identified in the public mind with the anti-Catholic
crusade as he had once been with the Populist movement."
That papists hardly constituted a homefront menace did not
deter Watson; even one Catholic was one too many, and be-
sides, he warned, rural Georgia did not lie beyond the clutches
of Rome.

On a semi-rational level Watson assailed the Church as a
danger to civil liberty and religious freedom, a familiar and
long-standing stock-in-trade of anti-Romanists. But readers
did not pore over Watson's *Jeffersonian Magazine* or *Jeffersonian Weekly* for informed analyses of church-state issues.
They thrived on the lurid and scurrilous "revelations" that
Watson dished out. The sexual gambolings of priests and
nuns were especially hot items among Watson's devotees, and
he larded his publications with lubricious tales. Typical fare
appeared in a piece in the *Jeffersonian Weekly* in 1912:

> Through his questions, the priest learns which of his fair pen-
> itents are inclined to indulge in sexual inclinations. Remember
> that the priest is often a powerfully sexed man, who lives on rich
> food, drinks red wine, and does no manual labor. He is alone with
> a beautiful, well-shaped young woman who tells him that she is
> tormented by carnal desire. Her low voice in his ear; the rustle of
> her skirts and the scent of her hair kindle flames. She will never
> tell what he says or does. She believes that *he* can forgive *her* sin.
> She has been taught in obeying *him,* she is serving God.

In 1920 Watson capped his career with election to the
United States Senate, the candidate of the same political
and economic establishment he had once so vociferously
challenged. His popularity had never been higher in Georgia, although one suspects that at least one segment of the
electorate—Georgia's handful of Catholics—absented itself
from the celebration.

V

When the Ku Klux Klan was reborn in 1915, in a ceremony atop Georgia's Stone Mountain, Tom Watson congratulated the founders and blessed the organization as a means to combat the Knights of Columbus. He did not live to see the Klan achieve its pinnacle, for he died in 1922, several years before the Klan peaked. Watson would have been proud had he lived, for in its heyday the Klan fashioned anti-Catholicism into an exquisite art. Catholic-baiting comprised only part of the Klan's bundle of hatreds, for it also savaged Jews, Negroes, immigrants, city dwellers and purveyors of immorality. It spread rapidly in the '20s, especially in the Southwest and Midwest, exercising an irresistible sway for a spell in Texas, Oklahoma and Indiana. For the Klan, Catholicism was part of an insidious menace to "100 Percent Americanism"; to battle Catholics was to strike a blow for the American Way. As followers of a foreign ruler, Catholics by definition could not be good Americans; "good Americans" were the Anglo-Saxon Protestants who dwelt on farms and in small towns in the South and Midwest. This appealed to Southerners; free at last of the stigma of treason, they could preen themselves as the quintessential Americans.

As far as Southern Catholics were concerned, the Klan barked a good deal more than it bit. But on occasion, it did bite. An especially deplorable instance of this occurred in Birmingham, Alabama, in 1921. Edwin R. Stephenson, a Protestant preacher, shot and killed Fr. James E. Coyle while the priest was sitting peaceably on the front porch of his rectory. Stephenson's act was in retaliation for Coyle's having performed a marriage ceremony between the preacher's daughter, a convert to Catholicism, and one Pedro Gussman, a Puerto Rican invariably described as "dark and curly-haired." Hugo Black, later of Supreme Court fame, and at the time a member of the Klan, conducted Stephenson's defense. Black played upon the jurors' fears of racial amalgamation and the Catholic menace, two specters guaranteed to inspire terror among God-fearing white folk. The Klan contributed money to the defense; the jury foreman was a Klansman, as was the chief of police who testified in Stephenson's behalf. Black won acquittal, and as a one-time Klansman remarked years later: "Hugo didn't have much trouble winning that verdict."

Despite such outrages, the Klan never provoked the kind of violence against Catholics that had led to such horrors as the Know-Nothing-inspired riots of the 1850s. Mainly, the South's Catholics laid low and kept quiet. In at least one case, they foiled the Klan with marvelous ingenuity. In the midst of the Klan's reign the Catholics of Nashville opened a new high school for boys; such a move was guaranteed to inflame bigots. In a brilliant stroke, one of the city's priests suggested to the bishop that he name the school after Fr. Abram Ryan, the much-celebrated "Poet of the Confederacy." As Thomas Stritch, the historian of the diocese, points outs, this was a "name venerated by Nashvillians and Tennesseans of all faiths," and to affix the famous priest's name to the school "would be a subtle and telling reminder that Catholicism had a much longer and infinitely nobler tradition than the Kluxers. . . ." The ploy worked; not only did Nashvillians welcome the school, but many Protestants contributed money to the bishop's building fund. Confederate nostalgia won hands down over anti-Catholicism.

VI

In part because of the Klan's campaign of nastiness, anti-Catholicism prospered in the 1920s. Even without the white-clad bigots, the '20s would have won recognition as perhaps the premier anti-Catholic decade in American history; only the 1840s and 1850s rival it. Southerners were especially prone to the disease, for they faced a bewildering array of problems, some of them directly linked to Catholicism, most not. In any case, Catholics furnished convenient scapegoats.

The Southern economy—dependent upon agriculture—wallowed in the doldrums in the 1920s. After a wartime premium on agricultural prices, the bottom dropped out of the farm market. While urban, industrial America basked in prosperity and hymned praises to progress, the rural South stagnated. American farmers had long ago accustomed themselves to an honored position in society. Thomas Jefferson had stated it succinctly: "Those who labor in the earth are God's chosen people. . . ." Tom Watson had invoked the farmers' loss of self-esteem to rally them in the 1880s and 1890s, another era of disastrously low crop prices. Not the Populist uprising, but a long season of boom times on the farm in the first two decades of the twentieth century, had restored the farmer's sense of well-being. In the '20s he found himself not only impoverished once again, but the butt of jokes and a figure of contempt among urban sophisticates. Jefferson's God-chosen farmer was now derided as "hick," "hayseed" and "rube." The Scopes trial of 1925 dramatized the clash between urban and rural America, between city refinement and country cloddishness.

The city symbolized everything that had gone haywire with America: industrialization, immigration, alien ideas, irreligiousness, immorality, mocking city-slickers. As the most rural region of the country, the South responded angrily to the situation. Cities bulged with immigrants, and, surmised the Southerner, these people, if not Jews, were Roman Catholics—teeming, wretched masses that threatened to subvert the verities the Southerner cherished. Baxter McLendon, a popular South Carolina evangelist, summarized the problem: Northern cities were filled with "a foreign brood of vultures with the smell of steerage on their carcasses that say we want the world to yield allegiance to Rome." Cities bristled with saloons (even though illegal), saloons with

Catholics—and Southerners, foursquare behind Prohibition, blamed Catholics for the evils of demon rum. Cities abounded with every vice imaginable, and their governments were hopelessly corrupt, travesties of the Founding Fathers' vision of republican government. And why not? In the Southern Protestant mind, vice and corruption were part and parcel of the decadent Roman Church.

Denizens of the rural South believed that their region formed the last bastion of an older and wholesome civilization. As long as the South had no big cities and few Catholics it could stave off destruction; that is, if it could maintain control of the blacks. Although white Southerners swore that blacks were happy in their subservience, there lurked a fear that something (a something that by definition would intrude from outside) would disturb this tranquillity. Here, too, the Catholic menace loomed. Out of the blue, Southerners seized upon the notion that the Catholic Church had undertaken to convert Southern blacks. Given the intense Protestantism of blacks, such a fear was a chimera, but chimeras can be more real than reality.

In a book published in 1927, *The New Challenge of Home Missions,* Eugene P. Alldredge, a high official in the Southern Baptist Sunday School Board, exposed Catholic designs. The Church evinced a "three-fold appeal" to blacks, Alldredge warned. In the first place, it promised to build "schools and still more schools" for them, and as every Southerner knew, an educated Negro was not a happy Negro. Even more pernicious, the Church permitted blacks to worship side by side with whites, thus encouraging the idea of equality. Finally, wrote Alldredge, childlike, superstitious blacks reveled in the mummery and mumbo-jumbo of Catholic ritual. Infestations of Polish, Italian and Irish Catholics in Yankee cities was one thing, but the prospect of black Catholics in the heart of Dixie raised a specter almost too hideous to contemplate.

Not content with agitating the South's blacks, the Church also threatened the equanimity of poor whites. Southerners arrived at this conclusion by linking Catholicism to labor unions. Other than sporadic outbreaks in the coal fields, the South had largely escaped the labor strife that accompanied industrialization. But in the late 1920s labor organizers swooped down upon Dixie, specifically to the textile mills of Virginia and the Carolinas. Not only did this threaten to drain the pool of cheap labor, but it also boded ill for the maintenance of racial segregation. What would happen if class became more important than race as the crucial division within Southern society? Southerners were aware of the Catholic Church's sympathies for labor unions, and they observed that muscular unions in the North depended upon a membership of Poles, Italians, Germans and Irishmen. Given the Southerner's taste for anti-Catholicism, it was easy for him to connect labor unrest with the designs of Rome.

Various preachers, peripatetic evangelists, journalists and politicians vied for the title of king of the Catholic-baiters. Senator Thomas J. Heflin of Alabama probably deserves the palm among politicians, even though he had many rivals within a profession that had learned from Tom Watson that tweaking the pope's nose was good politics. The ranks of men of the cloth supplied the most accomplished bigots. Among these, none surpassed the Reverend J. Frank Norris in the artistry, imaginativeness and sheer exuberance he brought to the war on Rome. As pastor of the First Baptist Church of Fort Worth, Texas, and a man of southwide influence, Norris was a worthy claimant to Watson's mantle. Like Watson, he stoked fears of Catholic subversion of religious liberty. But Norris, too, knew that folks ("the boys at the forks of the creeks," he called them) did not pay their money to hear reasoned discourses on church-state relations. They wanted entertainment, confirmation of their darkest suspicions, and a frisson to enliven the dull routines of plowing and planting, slopping hogs and milking cows. Norris eagerly complied.

He ferreted out plots within plots, conspiracies galore, and enough Catholic intrigues to fill a thick encyclopedia of anti-Catholicism. He was convinced, for example, that Catholics were trying to capture the city government of Fort Worth in order to silence his exposures of their Church's iniquities. Should they succeed, Norris wrote to an associate, "they would behead every Protestant preacher and disembowel every Protestant mother" in the city.

In good Watsonian fashion, Norris specialized in tales of clerical sexual escapades and in revelations of what went on behind the forbidding walls of convents. In his weekly newspaper, *The Fundamentalist,* he recommended "92 red hot books telling the inside truth of Roman Catholicism." Among the edifying volumes were *Jesuit Murders in the British Empire, Traffic in Nuns, Priest and Women, Crimes of Priests,* and, in a lighter vein, *The Anti-Catholic Joke Book.* It would be comforting to dismiss Norris as a sad case of mental derangement, but whatever strange monsters crawled through his brain, his fulminations struck a responsive chord among many Southerners, who were searching for explanations of what had gone wrong with their nation. Whether because of agreement or fear, few Southern voices were raised against Norris's hate-mongering.

VII

The anxiety, dread and anger orchestrated by Norris and his ilk roared to a crescendo in the presidential campaign of 1928. Alfred E. Smith, the Democratic party's nominee, personified to Southerners the sorry state of American civilization. Normally the South constituted the Democrats' "rotten borough," every four years trundling out the electoral apparatus to verify what everybody already knew: the "Solid South" voted Democratic as surely as the sun rises in the east; it had been so since the Civil War. In 1928 it appeared that the sun was about to rise in the west, for many Southerners found their candidate abhorrent. Smith was "wet"—in favor of repealing Prohibition; the South was dry. Smith was descended from Irish immigrants; the South was old-stock Anglo-Saxon. Smith hailed from New York City (and sounded like it), that Babylon-on-the-Hudson that epitomized moral degradation to upright farmers and town dwellers. Worst of all, Smith was a Catholic, who, in his capacity as governor, had personally welcomed a papal legate to New York City and reputedly had knelt and kissed the prelate's ring.

Some Southerners tried to keep the subject of Smith's religion on a relatively serious plane by raising questions about the Roman Church's teachings on civil and religious liberty. Such concerns were not illegitimate sixty years ago, at a time when the Church still officially viewed Protestants as "heretics." What about the papacy's historic conflict with civil rulers? Didn't the Church dominate the state in such places as Spain and Latin America, and use its favored position to persecute dissenters? Hadn't the Church made clear its disdain for democratic government? In the wake of the Second Vatican Council it is easy to dismiss such questions as excrescences of bigotry; in 1928 that was not necessarily the case. To give only one example: it was not simply bigotry that inspired a Baptist church in Florida to hold a series of classes during the campaign to discuss serious books on church-state relations. This same church invited Professor William Warren Sweet, America's most distinguished church historian at the time, to address the congregation on the topic.

Such temperateness was lost amidst the circus ringmastered by Frank Norris and his fellow impressarios. For Norris the situation was clear: Smith's nomination meant that "this nation at this present time is facing the greatest crisis of its existence." With the very survival of the American Way at stake, Norris and thousands of pastors and evangelists tumbled into the political arena to battle for the (Protestant) Lord. Talk of Catholic conspiracies was so rampant that a Catholic running for dogcatcher would have been denounced as part of a papal plot to seize control of the region's coon hounds. If

3. Catholic-Baiting with a Southern Accent 63

Smith were elected, Norris predicted, the White House would
be transformed into the Washington bureau of the Vatican.
He even suggested that Smith would, given the chance, un-
leash another St. Bartholomew's Day massacre.

A North Carolina ally of Norris discerned the intrigues
of the Knights of Columbus behind Smith's candidacy; the
Knights were, he averred, "the most vicious organization today
on earth." A poem (author unknown) that circulated in the
South during the campaign capsuled the attitude of many
Protestants. Entitled "Alcohol Smith's Platform," it married
poesy and bigotry in sublime union:

> I'll rule the people and the Pope will rule me,
> And the people's rights you will never see,
> And the Protestant heretics who vote for me,
> I'll reduce to abject slavery.
> I'll take down the flag from the public schools,
> And put up the cross for the ignorant fools.
> The Bibles in the schools will not be read,
> But instead we'll say masses for the dead.
> And the flag you love shall be put down,
> And put up instead the Papal crown;
> Then the Pope of Rome shall rule the homes,
> And bring back the glory that once was Rome's.

Al Smith lost to Herbert Hoover and Christian civilization
was saved, thanks in part to those Southerners who voted
Republican for the first (and probably last) time in their
life. Curiously, once having reached its zenith, rancorous and
vocal anti-Catholicism quickly subsided. Southern Protestants
did not suddenly become less hostile toward Catholicism,
but their obsession weakened; they talked about it less often
and less openly. Perhaps it was plain exhaustion from the
fever's climax; perhaps it was the realization that every scrap
of dirt against the Catholic Church had been dredged up
and made public. One hopes as well that there was—at least
among more sensible souls—embarrassment and disgust at the

anti-Catholic orgy that had surfeited the 1920s. Then, too, the onset of the Great Depression in 1930 propelled economic issues to the forefront; with massive economic ruin a reality, papal plots appeared of less moment.

The old beast could still roar at times—witness the outrage provoked by President Roosevelt's sending of a private envoy to the Vatican—but the Romanophobes never regained the fire and following of the golden age of Catholic-hating. Premillennialists continued to screech about the Whore of Babylon and Southern Protestants in general still flaunted the familiar combination of ignorance, anxiety and (often willful) misunderstanding of Catholicism, but never again would the South produce an anti-Catholicism of either the intensity or popularity of that which inflamed the region in the 1920s.

VIII

The ruckus raised by John F. Kennedy's Catholicism was small potatoes compared to the storm of '28. Opposition to Kennedy's religion existed in the South, but it never reached the proportions of the heyday of Romanophobia. Much had changed in the South since the 1920s. It had become less insular, more open to the outside world, and more thoroughly integrated into the nation as a whole. World War Two, with its defense industries and swollen military bases, brought jobs, economic opportunity and mobility. The South's cities embarked upon a season of growth that would boost them to primacy over the region's small towns and rural areas. Along with this came the beginnings of an economic boom that would transform the South in two decades or so into the Sun Belt, land of entrepreneurial dreams come true.

Prosperity brought newcomers to the South, many of whom were Catholics, and added ethnic and religious diversity to the population. Southerners who had scarcely laid eyes on a flesh-and-blood Catholic suddenly found themselves living next door to a whole family of them in the suburbs of, say, Atlanta, Richmond or Memphis. Young men who served in the armed forces in World War Two and the Korean War came into close contact with Catholics, and it is hard to hate the religion of a man with whom one has hunkered down in a foxhole. By 1960 Catholics were no longer quite so strange and threatening as granddaddy had warned.

Southerners felt less beleaguered and beseiged by 1960. Prosperity and economic promise planed the rough edges off the anxieties and defensiveness induced by privation and the struggle to survive. To a man who has been accustomed to few possessions, an automobile, a television set, a new boat and the jingle of spare change can do wonders for his outlook. The aversion to cities—a major source of disquietude in the '20s—gradually abated. The South's own urban areas were growing rapidly, fed by the country folk and small-towners flocking to the jobs and amenities they offered. The old bugaboo of Prohibition was gone, and no longer did the consumption of alcohol evoke images of drunken Catholic immigrants. Immigrants themselves had ceased to be an occasion of dread. The immigration acts of the 1920s had reduced the flow to a trickle, and the children and grandchildren of earlier arrivals were thoroughly Americanized by 1960. Al Smith's ties to the old country had raised suspicion in the South in 1928; John Kennedy's Irishness was endearing and colorful.

The most pressing concern in the South in 1960—from the white point of view—was the deterioration of racial harmony and the heightening of tensions between white and black. Montgomery had witnessed a successful bus boycott and Little Rock had watched paratroopers escort black children to Central High, but the turmoil of the '60s—a time of tumult that would again drive white Southerners into prickly insularity—had yet to engulf the South. Whatever dismay whites felt over the stirrings of blacks, they did not usually attempt—as some had in 1928—to blame it on the Catholic Church. The South's historic penchant for conspiracy theories did not much roil the waters when Kennedy waded in.

This does not mean that all was sweetness and light. Kennedy's religion *was* an issue among Southern Protestants, especially those of a fundamentalist persuasion. The same questions reappeared that had bedeviled Al Smith. Where did Kennedy's first loyalties lie? Suppose the pope were to order him to subvert the Constitution? Did Kennedy believe in the separation of church and state? The candidate chose to confront his detractors face to face by meeting with a conclave of preachers in Houston, Texas. Whether any minds were changed is problematic; Texas preachers do not easily surrender cherished prejudices. At the least, Kennedy displayed his sensitivity to Protestant concerns, and even hardrock Baptists found it difficult to resist JFK's charm and wit. Kennedy did not banish the religious issue at Houston, but he defused it—at least on the level of respectable and reasoned discourse.

As usual, the unrespectable and unreasoned flourished. The regular characters slithered out from under rocks to enlighten the Southern electorate about Catholicism. Premillennialists sang the old tune about the Whore of Babylon and fundamentalists bellowed about papal plots. Handbills appeared on telephone poles and automobile windshields to warn of dark doings in Rome. Tales of convent capers made the rounds once again, and the Jesuit-as-conspirator resurfaced. Somehow, though, it just wasn't the same as in the good old days. To be sure, one could easily find people who credited such balderdash, and vestigial animosities welled in many a Southern breast. But the scale and intensity did not measure up to the Catholic-hating of yore. Call it greater sophistication, call it enlightenment or apathy, but whatever the explanation, the Catholic-baiters could not evoke the fervor their predecessors had summoned.

John Kennedy as Catholic President was not demonstrably different than John Kennedy as Protestant would have been.

Little wonder, for as we subsequently discovered, he wasn't a very good Catholic anyhow. Even those Southerners who had warned most grimly of what would happen if a papist ever got his hands on the levers of power had to admit that Kennedy did not turn the government over to the Vatican, nor even install a coterie of Jesuits in the White House. Once it had happened—once a Catholic had actually made it to the top—it was hard to recall what all the fuss had been about. Whatever Kennedy's faults, he did largely dispel the Catholic issue from Southern politics. When Walter Mondale selected the Catholic Geraldine Ferraro as his running mate in 1984 one had to search diligently to find people exercised about papal plots and Jesuit cabals. Politically, anti-Catholicism was moribund, if not stone dead, in the South.

IX

Coincident with Kennedy's presidency, the Second Vatican Council began to soften many of the fears that had once tormented the Southern Protestant brain. Even fundamentalists found it difficult to discern malignancy behind the kindly, smiling countenance of Pope John XXIII; he looked too much like someone's granddaddy to be suspect. His council induced changes that did not go unnoticed in the South. The forthright acceptance of freedom of religion eased Protestant hostility, as did the new talk of "separated brethren" instead of "heretics." The switch to the vernacular in the Mass and the tendency to dispense with, or at least to downplay, such things as bells, candles, incense and holy water lessened the creepy-mysterious atmosphere that had so disconcerted people accustomed to starkly plain Baptist and Church of Christ worship services.

Nuns ceased to parade around in weird outfits and started dressing like normal ladies (and thereby settled a long-standing dispute: yes, they did have hair on their head).

Priests proved to be regular folks, not the least because so many of them exchanged their black suits and dog collars for sport shirts (usually of execrable taste) and slacks. Democratic urges worthy of Baptists belied the standard image of Catholic authoritarianism. Catholics took to singing "Amazing Grace" and "A Mighty Fortress," and though they did not do it very well, their intentions were obviously wholesome. At least those odious chants—the kind that made a Protestant's skin crawl—were gone. The doors of a hermetic institution were flung open, and Protestants could peek inside and see that, after all, it was not so very exotic—and certainly not un-American.

One can argue that Vatican II has had a deleterious effect upon American Catholicism, but it cannot be gainsaid that it has favorably altered the Southern Protestant's opinion of the Catholic Church. After the Council, a Southerner could feel comfortable with Catholicism in a way that he could not before. The two Johns—Kennedy and XXIII—did not erase anti-Catholicism from the South, but they—along with the social and economic changes that had occurred since World War Two—robbed it of its vitality. Frank Norris and Tom Watson would have been aghast.

4. It's a Long, Hard Road from Dixieland to Rome

A curious thing about the twentieth-century South: at once the most vociferously anti-Catholic region of the United States, it has lost some of its most illustrious sons and daughters to the hated Roman Church. Catholicism has exhibited an especially strong attraction for the South's intellectuals and imaginative writers. The list is distinguished: Allen Tate, Caroline Gordon, Katherine Anne Porter, Tennessee Williams, Walker Percy. Others felt the pull of Rome, but resisted. The poet and critic Donald Davidson, for example, reportedly was taking instruction in the Catholic faith at the time of his death in 1968; Thomas Stritch, a native of Nashville who knew Davidson, writes that he "came to the threshold of Catholicism without making the final step. . . ." Davidson's daughter, herself a convert, arranged for his burial in the Catholic cemetery in Nashville. Davidson's fellow poet in the Agrarian movement, John Gould Fletcher, flirted briefly with the Church in the 1930s. The Roman temptation retains its seductiveness. In the mid-1970s the prominent Vanderbilt novelist and critic Walter Sullivan converted, and more recently, the novelist Mary Lee Settle, now a Virginian, but originally from West Virginia, entered the Church.

Given the South's militant Protestantism and its record of anti-Catholicism, conversion would appear an unlikely option for Southerners. By becoming a Catholic the Southerner takes a drastic step. He joins a Church whose culture and traditions are rooted in the Mediterranean and Latin lands, rather than in the Scotland, England and Ulster from which his ancestors migrated to America. Even today Catholicism has not lost the coloration given to it by successive waves of immigration that, since the early nineteenth century, have brought millions of Irish, Germans, Poles, Italians and Hispanic peoples to the United States. Culturally, the Southern convert finds himself submerged in a sea of heterogeneous people alien to his own background.

The Southern convert opens a chasm between himself and his region and people. The Catholic Church is still not fully accepted in the South; it is a "Northern" institution, and the recent migration of Catholics to the Sun Belt only sharpens that identification. The South remains the most self-conscious section of America; history made it different, and this distinctiveness has shaped its people. In converting to Catholicism one rejects part of that identity, namely the Protestantism that lies at the heart of what it means to be a Southerner. In the South, family—the extended ties of kith and kin—has always exercised powerful (some would say tyrannical) sway over the individual. Each family is rooted in a particular denomination; one is a Baptist, say, or Methodist or Presbyterian more for historical reasons than out of conscious choice. To repudiate the faith of one's ancestors is more than a religious decision; it entails, in a sense, a rejection of family as well. More than one Southern convert has felt the sting of a family reaction that runs the gamut from outrage, shock and dismay to sorrow and pity.

II

Despite these hazards, Southerners *have* converted, even before Allen Tate and some of his fellow writers of the Southern literary Renascence of the 1920s and 1930s made it almost stylish to do so. Take, for example, Francis Asbury Baker, the son of a prominent Baltimore physician, and, as his given names indicate, heir to a long family tradition of Methodism. (Francis Asbury was the first Methodist bishop in the United States.) After graduating from Princeton in 1839, Baker became an Episcopalian and then a clergyman in that church. This was acceptable, for Episcopalianism has always been the main religion of the gentry in the South. After winning fame as a preacher, Baker converted to Catholicism in 1853, and three years later, took the vows of the Redemptorist order. In 1858 he joined Fr. Isaac Hecker, a convert from New England, in founding the Paulists. None of this was acceptable, and Baker's tergiversation scandalized Baltimore's polite Protestant circles.

Baker's fellow Marylander, Samuel Eccleston, also took the road to Rome in the antebellum era. Born on the Eastern Shore in 1801, he began life as a Presbyterian. When his father died, his mother remarried, this time to a Catholic, who influenced young Samuel to join the Church. Eccleston was ordained in 1825, became a Sulpician, and was appointed president of his alma mater, St. Mary's College in 1829. Five years later he became archbishop of Baltimore, a position he held until his death in 1851.

In Virginia the Church won two well-known figures in the pre-Civil War years. John Floyd was one of the state's most distinguished political leaders of the 1820s and 1830s. A prominent physician, he was elected to Congress in 1817 and held the seat for the next twelve years. He capped his political career by serving as governor from 1830 to 1834. Midway through his term he converted to Catholicism, an act that caused a stir in the Old Dominion, a state unaccustomed to Catholic governors.

Andrew Monroe was of *the* Monroes and nephew to the President. Born and raised in Charlottesville, he won appointment to the Naval Academy and was commissioned in the Navy in time to serve in the war with Mexico. In 1853 he did the unthinkable: he joined the Catholic Church. A year later he resigned from the Navy and entered the Society of Jesus. He was ordained in 1860, and from then until his death fourteen years later he taught at St. Francis Xavier College in New York City.

North Carolina, as usual, had to play second fiddle to Virginia, but it did claim at least one eminent convert. Levi Silliman Ives was not a native Southerner, but he was appointed Episcopal bishop of North Carolina. Active in the High Church movement, he became increasingly dissatisfied with the Anglican communion. His search for a church with an authority that would withstand all tests led him in the 1850s to switch to the Roman Church, thereby confirming the worst fears of opponents of High Church Anglicanism.

Lucius Bellinger Northrop belonged to a leading South Carolina family. He attended West Point, entered the Army, and became a close friend to young Jefferson Davis. Northrop's later conversion to Catholicism did not shock Davis, for Davis himself had been educated at a Catholic school in Kentucky and had felt the tug of Rome as a youth. When Davis became President of the Confederate States of America he appointed his old friend to the post of commissary general of the Southern armies.

III

The trickle of conversions continued after the Civil War. Perhaps the most famous was General James Longstreet. Conversion to Catholicism in 1877 completed Longstreet's abandonment of the dominant ethos of his native land. Although he was one of the South's most talented generals during the war, his career ended under a cloud, for many Southerners blamed him for the debacle at Gettysburg. Longstreet remained bitter over this accusation for the rest of his life. He earned further obloquy by joining the Republican party, a betrayal of the worst sort to Southerners suffering the ignominy of defeat and occupation by a Union Army that took its marching orders from Republicans in Washington. Next to this, Longstreet's conversion to Catholicism was of little consequence to his fellow Southerners.

Later in the century Tennesseans were startled to see one of their most promising young men go over to the Catholic Church. John Marks Handly was the nephew of a governor of Tennessee. After graduating from the newly founded Vanderbilt University in the 1880s he left his homeland for New York City, where he launched a career in journalism. He became private secretary to the Louisiana novelist George Washington Cable, and moved to Northampton, Massachusetts, where Cable had taken up exile because of the unpopularity in Louisiana of his views on race relations. Here Handly became friends with a group of Paulist priests, and in 1895 he joined the Church. Following his ordination as a Paulist in 1899, he returned to Tennessee. He persuaded his order to purchase a mansion that had been built near Winchester by his cousin. Handly and several other priests converted the house into a retreat center and a locus of Catholic missionizing, a role it played until the 1950s. Through the work of Fr. Handly and his successors, the Winchester area in south-central Tennessee has one of the state's largest concentrations of Catholics outside of the major cities.

The postbellum South also witnessed the beginnings of a phenomenon that would become more common in the following century: the conversion of literary figures. The first of these was John Bannister Tabb, a name now familiar only to scholars, but in the decade and a half before his death in 1909, a poet of notable reputation. Tabb was born in 1845 to a Virginia plantation family in Amelia County south of Richmond. Weak eyesight kept him out of the Confederate Army, but it did not prevent him from enlisting with a blockade-runner. In 1864 the Federals captured his ship and imprisoned him at Point Lookout, Maryland, an infamous prison whose brutalities have been unjustly overshadowed by the outrage of Andersonville, the Confederate prison in Georgia. After the war Tabb settled in Baltimore, where he taught piano at a boys' school. He became friends with Alfred Curtis, then an Episcopal clergyman, but one with strong proclivities toward Rome. Curtis turned Tabb to religion, and in 1872 both men converted to Catholicism. (Curtis later became bishop of Wilmington, Delaware.) Tabb eventually followed his friend into holy orders, receiving ordination in 1884. From then until 1907, when blindness forced his retirement, he taught at St. Charles College near Baltimore.

Richard Malcolm Johnston was born in Georgia in 1822, son of a planter who was also a Baptist preacher. After graduating from Mercer University Johnston by turns taught school and practiced law until 1857, when he won appointment as professor of rhetoric and belles lettres at the University of Georgia. When the coming of the war shut down the institution, Johnston opened a school for boys and spent the war years eking out an existence by teaching. In 1867 he moved to Baltimore and opened a private school. Prodded by his friend, the poet Sidney Lanier, he began to devote more time to the stories he had been composing on droll happenings in antebellum rural Georgia. This avocation became a vocation when, after his conversion to Catholicism in 1875, the Baptist parents who formed his clientele yanked their sons from his school. Although Johnston benefited from the vogue in Northern magazines for tales of the Old South, he never earned enough to support his family adequately. But he continued to write short stories, sketches and novels until his death in 1898.

Neither Tabb nor Johnston attained to the first rank of Southern letters in the late nineteenth century. That distinction belonged to their friend Sidney Lanier and to such poets as Paul Hamilton Hayne and Henry Timrod. Even more important were the prose writers Joel Chandler Harris, Thomas Nelson Page, George Washington Cable and, the most famous Southern writer of the era, Mark Twain. In winning Tabb and

Johnston, the Church did not gain the sort of literary figure who commanded great fame or who could influence others toward Rome by example. (Harris, an immensely popular writer, did become a Catholic, but just barely: he slipped under the wire with a deathbed conversion.) That would change dramatically in the half century after World War One, when the Church would attract a number of the leading writers of the South. It does not overstate the case to suggest that in the twentieth century the most distinguished and famous converts in the South have come from the ranks of literary artists. The Church has exercised no appeal for the Southern masses; only the creative and intellectual elite has responded.

IV

Why does anyone convert to the Church? G. K. Chesterton, himself a convert, remarked in *The Catholic Church and Conversion* that the Church has a hundred doors; each person finds his own, knocks and enters. One might say a thousand doors or ten thousand, for each individual's experience is unique. If all were the same, the enduring popularity—for writer and reader alike—of spiritual autobiographies would long ago have declined into boredom with a repetitious tale. From Augustine's *Confessions* to the latest narrative, the story has retained its vibrant freshness.

The convert often prefers to view the matter as an elementary fact of perception: he perceives that Roman Catholicism is true and then acts upon that shock of recognition. But how many conversions can be reduced to such simplicity? Man is a many-faceted and complicated creature; rarely can his motivation be reduced to a single, unambiguous cause. *Credo*, yes: but behind that lies much else.

For some, Rome provides a rock-solid authority that they miss in their Protestant or unbelieving life. They want answers, and the Catholic Church has traditionally furnished them without equivocation. At its worst, this desire for authority arises from weariness with thinking and choosing; at best, it stems from a longing for certitude in a world of flux, changing standards of truth and debilitating relativism. It does not invalidate the act to observe that the authority-seeker forms a mother lode for the picks and shovels of psychologizers. The term "Mother Church" exudes enough connotations and implications to dizzy a Freudian with delight.

The Church is also a life preserver thrown to a drowning man. Whether the incidence of despair has taken a quantum leap in the twentieth century is a debatable—and unverifiable—proposition. Suffice it to say, our era engenders good and objective reasons for hopelessness; the man of despair has become a stock figure on the cultural scene. He seeks surcease from his anguish in a variety of ways: sex, drugs, wealth, power, career, travel, violence. All these can for a time ease the ache of emptiness. But the reckoning comes: stripped of his defenses and all his nerve-benumbing anodynes, the despairing soul staggers to the brink to stare into the abyss. Many a Catholic convert has stood on this precipice, gazed down in preparation to leap, and seen there, in the darkness of the pit, a small candle—faint and flickering, perhaps, but still casting the light that has emanated from it for two thousand years. And a voice whispers: "Take up this candle and see, for I am the Light of the World."

Scores of Protestants and unbelievers have entered the Church because it offers water to souls parched by the sereness of modern life. This is an emotional response, evoked by the Church's pageantry, drama, colorful ritual and inspiring liturgy—the "smells and bells" that Protestants observe with a tantalizing mixture of fear, revulsion, awe and attraction. Science, technology and rationalism have steadily eroded the mystery of existence since the seventeenth century. Man needs mystery—his being does not live by reason and intellect alone—and he will find it wherever he can. The ubiquitous newspaper horoscope attests to the continuing allure of astrology. Fraternal lodges, honorary societies, and college Greek-letter organizations indulge in candles, decorative banners, secret signs and liturgically exact initiation rites. UFOs provide the necessary element for some, while others turn to Eastern religions and the occult for relief from the blandness of advanced technological society. For those who seek a more traditional outlet, Protestantism—save for sky-High Anglicanism—offers little. The starkness and studied plainness of most Protestant churches occupy the flip-side of the scientific-technological-rationalistic coin.

But Roman Catholicism: ah, there's a faith with mystery enough to quench the thirst of the most desiccated soul. It has it all: saints to beseech; the Eternal Feminine, personified by the Virgin; mystic union with God; martyrs' bones, holy relics, liquifying blood, stigmata, the Shroud of Turin; and a heaven, hell and purgatory palpable enough to inspire a Florentine poet to compose a sublime comedy. Strangely garbed nuns, black-clad priests and the manifold secrets of the cloister—these, too, heighten the effect. Add the darkened confessional, holy water, incense, candles, genuflections, multi-colored vestments, and, until recently, an exotic Latin tongue. Nor should one overlook the most immense mystery of all: bread transformed into flesh, wine converted to blood. There is more than enough to replenish the wells of mystery depleted by three centuries of science, technology, rationalism and skepticism.

V

These broad considerations establish a backdrop for an analysis of Catholicism's appeal to the Southern writer. The next step is to highlight the particularities of the writer's experience. A cynical quip by the critic Philip Rahv furnishes a good place to begin. In the late 1940s, at a time when many writers—not just Southern ones—were heading toward Rome,

Rahv opined that they were searching for "new metaphors."
Rahv had no patience with the converts, but out of disdain,
he spoke more truly than he realized.

Metaphor implies that everything in God's creation is related. The *Song of Songs* resonates with a metaphorical richness that beholds oneness in creation: "As the lily among
thorns, so is my love among the daughters"; "thy two breasts
are like two young roes that are twins, which feed among
the lillies." All created things are related, and all find their
ultimate meaning in unity with God. To quote Flannery
O'Connor (borrowing from Teilhard de Chardin): "Everything that rises must converge."

Yahweh uttered the Word and creation sprang from the
formless void. From that creation, the writer draws his images,
images that descend from the hand of God; in using them, the
writer *ascends* toward God. His art puts him in touch with
the spirit of creation that throbs throughout the cosmos.

The Southern writer has pursued his art in a culture per-
meated with a Protestantism that harbors strong suspicions
toward the created world. In its most pronounced form, this
debouches into a Manichaean hatred of the physical world
because it is evil. Flesh and spirit war with one another, the
flesh striving to drag the spirit into the mire of temporality,
the spirit struggling to escape the corruption of the flesh. The
typical Southern house of worship is, for example, stark and
barren inside, though, incongruously, it may sport a Gothic
exterior. Denuded of embellishment, it reveals a mistrust of
the senses and of the plenitude of creation. Sin corrupts all;
man's task is to shun the world and escape the clutches of
evil. We are pilgrims trudging through a vale of tears on our
way to glory. A chasm yawns between heaven and earth; Satan
rules below, God above.

Metaphor is suspect, especially when it embraces the ana-
gogical. Nothing on this earth is *like* anything in the timeless
realm of eternity. Human, fleshly love, for example, is not an
emblem of divine love; temporal love is corrupt, vitiated by

sin, debased by lust. This imposes on the writer a truncated vision; it prevents him from ascending to the divine through the senses. On the one side lie the beauties of the natural world, but to revel in these is to confess one's corruption. On the other side is the realm of spirit, but, severed from nature, this is desiccated, cut off from the life-giving blood of the world's body. Protestantism, in its typical Southern manifestation, spurns art and distrusts the artist.

At its best, Catholicism offers a different perspective. *At its best:* this is the operative phrase, for the best has often been obscured by a world-blasting Jansenism. This is especially germane to the Church in America, for since the middle of the nineteenth century American Catholicism has been saturated with a Jansenism imported by the Irish priests who followed their flocks to this country in the 1840s, and who continued to be enlisted, well into the twentieth century, to staff undermanned parishes.

The Southern writer was in an advantageous position to perceive only the best side of Catholicism. Because he did not live in a region dominated by Irish-American Catholicism, he was not forced to equate Jansenism with the faith. The Catholicism he perceived was not that of Fr. O'Connor and the folks of St. Brendan's parish, but rather the historic Catholicism that sweeps across the centuries of Western civilization and projects a grand and sublime tradition of high drama, of heroes, saints, adventurers, warriors—and artists. Had he confronted Catholicism in the quotidian reality of parish existence, he would not have been drawn to it, for he would have discovered a Jansenist ambience that shared much with the creation-hating fundamentalism of the South. By virtue of standing outside the culture of the Church in America, he could grasp Catholic tradition in its fullness, and let his imagination be stimulated by the historic romance of the faith.

The Southern writer had another advantage: he did not come from a society infested with the secularity of modernism.

Even though he did not cotton to the fundamentalism of his native region, he often disclosed a decidedly religious bent. As Flannery O'Connor remarked, he was likely to be at least "Christ-haunted." How could he help but be? Until the South launched its leap into full modernity after World War Two, the writer was born and raised in a society suffused with Christianity. It was as much a part of his world as the unforgiving sun that beat upon him in the long, languid summers. It was a given. The Southern writer was drunk on words, and as a child he had imbibed the intoxicating brew of the King James Bible, the wellspring of the Southern religious experience.

Religion was in the marrow of his bones—which is not to say that he was necessarily *religious.* Unless he felt some vague attachment to the aesthetic delights of Episcopalianism (and in the South even Episcopalianism offers little of that, for it is adamantly Low Church in outlook), he probably professed no religion at all. To the godly folk around him, he appeared godless. And he might be: he might have succeeded in cleansing himself of every speck of the religion of the South. But I doubt it. More likely, he fitted O'Connor's description. Most writers of the Southern Renascence—those who came of age between roughly 1920 and 1960—fall into the category of "Christ-haunted." Faulkner and Robert Penn Warren, to name two, might have supplied the model for Miss O'Connor's typology.

For some, the ghost of Christian belief was too strong to be held at bay. Such a person found himself drawn ineluctably— perhaps reluctantly as well—toward another identity that O'Connor singled out, one that described her own spiritual condition: "Christ-centered." What to do? Homegrown Protestantism (or any imported varieties either) would not suffice. Lo and behold, there stood the most improbable option of all: Roman Catholicism. At least a few of these God-seeking writers surrendered to the improbable.

As a God-seeker he discovered in the Church a truth that

answered his most deeply felt spiritual needs. But as an artist he found something else: a religion that enhanced and encouraged his art. It *did—pace* Philip Rahv—furnish him with new metaphors. Its imagery-rich liturgy quickened his imagination and heightened his senses. In the Mass he knelt before a priest who held aloft the wafer and cup and said: "This is the body and blood of Christ." Not merely a pale symbol, as Protestants would have it, but *is*. Spirit and flesh become one; the chasm is bridged: all things are one, and all are in Christ. The creation is not corrupt; distorted by sin, yes, but still *good*. Not revulsion at creation, but rejoicing in its divine imprint, enwrapped him. His art was not at war with corrupt nature; rather it celebrated God's presence in a fallen world. He did not have to choose between God and art; as a Catholic he could have both. In a sense they are one, not because art is religion (a misconception propagated by the Romantics), but because man's art partakes of the divine artistry that suffuses creation.

VI

Unfortunately, one cannot prove that this dynamic of conversion occurred in the minds and souls of Southern writers, for the irreducible fact is that none of them composed a spiritual autobiography that spells out the particulars of conversion. I do not contend that the convert consciously articulated all of these things even to himself; religion rarely works that way in any case. I do believe, however, that in the depths of his being he understood something similar to what I have adumbrated. But even without the insight of spiritual autobiography, one can piece together some of the elements that led individual Southern writers to convert to Catholicism.

Katherine Anne Porter joined the Church in 1910 when she was twenty years old; her age at conversion distinguishes her from her fellow converts on the Southern literary scene, for most of them waited until later in life to embrace the faith. Because Porter indulged habitually in a prevarication that far exceeded the usual authorial penchant for readjusting reality to suit oneself (in other words, she lied heroically), it is difficult to penetrate her motives. Her biographer, Joan Givner, offers this insight:

> . . . There was a great deal that appealed to her aesthetic sense. She loved the dramatic qualities of the Mass, the beauty of the liturgy, the sound of the church music and the Latin words. She liked the atmosphere of the churches, with their ornate windows, high altars, intricate vestments, and she was moved by the symbolism inherent in word and gesture.

Is this simply a case of the smells-and-bells syndrome? Perhaps, but it cuts deeper. It hints at what I suggested earlier: the power of the Church to provide a solution to the uneasy condition of Christ-hauntedness.

Whatever Porter's reasons for joining the Church, her sojourn in it was stormy. If nothing else, her astonishing randiness—mother to countless sexual liaisons—would have hindered her from conformity with Church teaching. Beyond that, as Givner remarks: "She was not likely to be an orthodox Catholic anymore than an orthodox anything else." She nursed a lifelong proclivity for fault-finding, disagreement and discontent. Throughout her life she regularly drifted away from the Church and then, just as predictably, wandered back through its doors. New acquaintances, catching her in the "out" part of the cycle, were invariably startled to learn she was a Catholic. Yet priests and nuns always found her "very devout," according to Givner, "and they never questioned her strong faith." In religion, as in everything else, Katherine Anne Porter was a very confused woman.

This appears in an incident recounted by Flannery O'Connor in a letter of 1958. She had earlier met and liked Porter, and when Porter came to Macon to give a reading, O'Connor invited her to lunch at the O'Connor farm near

Milledgeville. During the meal, Porter inquired about a forth-
coming trip that O'Connor and her mother were planning.
O'Connor replied that they were making a pilgrimage to
Lourdes. According to O'Connor,

> . . . A very strange expression came over her face, just a slight
> shock as if some sensitive spot had been touched. She said that
> she had always wanted to go to Lourdes, perhaps she would get
> there some day and make a novena.

The conversation then turned to whimsical repartee about
death. Porter, noted O'Connor,

> . . . Said she thought it was very nice to believe that we would
> all meet in heaven and she rather hoped we would but she didn't
> really know. She wished she knew who exactly was in charge of
> this universe, and where she was going. She would be glad to go
> where she was expected if she knew.

Toward the end of her long life the confusion cleared; the
prospect of one's own death *does* concentrate the mind. Givner
remarks that "during the last years . . . Porter found her greatest consolation in the Church." Two nuns from Baltimore visited her regularly in these years (Porter was living then near
Washington, D.C.), and a priest came periodically to hear her
confession and to give her the Eucharist. Toward the end, she
told one of the nuns: "Death is beautiful. I long to die. I love
God. I know that he loves me." Whatever her motives for en-
tering the Church, and however tempestuous had been her
relations with it, did not matter: she died in the faith.

VII

If anyone was more confused about God, man and the cosmos than Porter, it was Tennessee Williams. Williams's boy-
hood hero was his maternal grandfather, an Anglo-Catholic

clergyman in Mississippi, and Williams retained an enduring respect for the Episcopal Church. At an anti-war rally in the Cathedral of St. John the Divine in New York City in 1975 Williams angrily stormed out of the church during the performance of an obscenity-laden play by Norman Mailer; Williams was irate at such desecration. When Williams was seventeen his grandfather took him on a tour of Europe. During the trip Williams suffered a nervous breakdown, a shattering experience that was relieved only when the tormented youth stumbled into the cathedral in Cologne, fell upon his knees, and begged God to heal him. He felt an "impalpable hand" touch his head, and in that instant, the terrors fled. In the 1970s Williams told his friend Dotson Rader: "At seventeen I had no doubt at all that the hand of our Lord Jesus had touched my head with mercy. . . ."

Neither his grandfather's influence nor the Episcopal Church could save Williams from a destructive descent into drugs, alcohol, degrading homosexual promiscuity and nervous collapses. In 1969, in the midst of one of Williams's most horrific mental breakdowns, his brother Dakin, himself a convert to Catholicism, arrived at Williams's home in Key West, carted him to a priest and had him baptized. In Williams's later retellings the episode hovers between slapstick comedy and strong-armed coercion. Williams's most authoritative biographer, Donald Spoto, illuminates the nature of the "conversion." Dakin contacted a Jesuit, Fr. Joseph LeRoy, who agreed to talk with Tennessee. Spoto recounts that "in reply to Father LeRoy's questions [Williams] said that he was indeed in despair, that he wanted to have his goodness restored, that he wanted to find God. . . ." Fr. LeRoy later told Spoto that "I found Tenn an eager listener." Spoto exonerates both the priest and Dakin from any undue haste or even subtle coercion:

. . . He [Williams] submitted with the casual carelessness of the drugged to the spiritual ministrations offered to him. Neither his brother nor the clergyman could assume anything other than his willingness to find consolation and challenge from the life of faith. . . .

The conversion did not stick, but neither was it the "joke" Williams sometimes called it. Williams, too, was one of O'Connor's "Christ-haunted" Southerners. In his bedroom in his Key West house he erected an "altar" atop a card table. It held a jumble of items, including a picture of his mentally deranged sister Rose, statues of Vishnu and the Virgin and Child, and a picture of St. Jude. This was not homosexual "camp," for Rader comments that Williams "sometimes prayed here, when he was frightened or lonely. . . ." Spoto remarks that Williams considered himself and Rose to be "hopeless cases," hence the picture of St. Jude. "Such cases exist," Williams once said; "we know that, so what can we do but pray?"

Williams died on February 25, 1983, choking to death on a bottle cap that, in his alcoholic and drugged stupor, he mistook for a pill. On the nightstand next to his deathbed there was, according to Rader, "a small triptych showing the Virgin and Child, an object he carried with him when he traveled."

Was Tennessee Williams a Catholic? Certainly not by any normal definition of that term. But he *was* baptized into the Church, and during his sordid life, grace seemed always to be playing at the edges of his heart, searching for an entry into the center of his being. He knew that neither money, fame, sex nor mind-numbing drugs and alcohol could dispel the "cold wind around my heart that wraps me in despair." I, for one, would be unwilling to consign Williams to the legion of the damned. The mystery of salvation is impenetrable, and who knows what transpired between God and Williams in that last moment when the woebegone, tormented playwright gasped his final breath?

VIII

No one ever accused Allen Tate of being confused. He was the brainiest, most articulate literary intellectual produced by the South in its history. Unfortunately, his articulateness did not extend very far into the realm of personal religion; although he too converted to Catholicism, he never wrote about it in a direct way. Yet a perusal of his writings, supplemented by facets of his life, offers some clues. Tate's case illustrates the relationship between Catholicism and the search for authority, or, to put it in specifically Southern terms, the quest for something to replace the attenuated traditions of the Southern past.

As a student at Vanderbilt in the early 1920s Tate was neither self-consciously Southern nor especially concerned with the preservation of tradition. He was indubitably a Southerner; born and raised in Kentucky, he had, in addition, imbibed from his mother a strong attachment to the land of her family, the Chesapeake region of Maryland and Virginia. But at Vanderbilt Tate was more the self-conscious modern poet than anything else. One of his classmates later recalled a familiar scene: Allen Tate striding across the campus with a volume of T. S. Eliot tucked under his arm. Eliot and the modernist masters, not the ragged men in grey, were Tate's heroes in the early '20s.

Tate soon headed for New York City to begin an apprenticeship in literary journalism and to win his spurs as a poet. Like many young men and women of his day, he gladly put the provinces behind him to partake of the abundant intellectual feast available in the nation's cultural capital. Here one could discard the tacky mental attire of countryside and small town and garb oneself in the stylish dress of sophistication and cosmopolitanism. Sinclair Lewis, though older than the young exiles, voiced their disdain for the drab hinterland. Lewis launched his fame in 1920 with *Main Street,* a novel that exposed the small town in all its backwardness, pettiness and boorish self-satisfaction. Two years later he followed with *Babbitt*, a portrait of provincial boosterism and commercialization of values. George Babbitt's Zenith, Ohio, could have been Nashville, Tennessee, an aggressive New South city where Babbitt's Southern cousins burbled about progress, growth and development. Lewis's third blockbuster, *Elmer Gantry* (published in 1927), pilloried the preacher as con artist, the religious counterpart to *Babbitt*'s man-on-the-make.

This was a bad time for religion, especially of the Southern variety. In 1925 the East Tennessee town of Dayton hosted the Scopes trial, an event that—with the help of H. L. Mencken's dispatches from the front—made Tennessee and the South the source of merriment in such places as New York City. Tate must have cringed in those days when cocktail-chat turned to the "gaping primates" and barefoot fundamentalists of Tennessee. He did something more than to shrink from the gibes of his amused friends, though: he began to rethink the matter of Southernness. Like his former professors at Vanderbilt—notably John Crowe Ransom and Donald Davidson—Tate took umbrage at the mockery aimed at his homeland. Among Tate and like-minded Southern intellectuals, a hair-trigger defensiveness emerged: Those Tennessee fundamentalists might be dumb rednecks, but they are *our* dumb rednecks and not to be subjected to sport among smart-aleck Yankee intellectuals.

Aversion to Yankee barbs soon issued in exultation at being a Southerner. Tate, Ransom, Davidson and others of the Vanderbilt circle embraced self-conscious Southernness and bodied forth a defiant pride in their region. But this was not enough to silence Yankee scoffers; the need for an aggressive counterattack was apparent. Out of this realization came the Agrarian movement and the symposium of 1930, *I'll Take My Stand: The South and the Agrarian Tradition*. Tate, Ransom and Davidson were the moving spirits behind the volume, and

together they collected nine other kindred souls, among whom
were Robert Penn Warren, Andrew Lytle, Stark Young, Frank
Owsley and John Donald Wade.

The book announced a two-fold purpose: defense of the
South, and celebration of its "agrarian tradition," the last bastion in America, as the essayists saw it, of the time-tested values of Western civilization. The Vanderbilt circle pitted the
agrarian South against the urbanized, industrialized North;
tradition against modernity; stability and continuity against
flux and innovation; hearth and home, family and kinship
ties, and respect for religion against the rootless, deracinated
secularized life of the North. "Agrarianism" became their ral-
lying cry, and during the 1930s they engaged their antagonists
(which included as many Southerners as Northerners) in combat through books, articles and platform debates. Tate and his
colleagues transformed the Backward South into the Militant
South.

Tate committed himself wholeheartedly to the venture; convinced that Southern tradition provided meaning to life in the
twentieth century, he dedicated his dazzling intellect and fe-
licitous pen to its defense. "Convinced" may be too strong;
perhaps it is more accurate to say that Tate was searching for
meaning in the modern world and settled upon Southern tradition as the answer. "Settled upon" may be too unequivocal
as well, for Tate was uneasy. His contribution to *I'll Take My
Stand,* entitled "Remarks on the Southern Religion," indicates
as much.

Rather than a straightforward examination of religion in
the South, this essay is a devilishly knotty meditation on history, religion and metaphysics. Explicators of the Agrarian
symposium usually tiptoe past this piece; no one seems completely sure of what Tate was driving at. Despite the opacity of the essay, one thing is certain: Tate was not entirely
comfortable with Southern tradition. To many of his fellow symposiasts, the Old South—the South before the Civil
War—embodied their version of the Golden Age. Tate de-
murred, faulting the antebellum South as "a feudal society

without a feudal religion." The problem lay, Tate argued, in the region's attempt to "encompass its destiny within the terms of Protestantism, in origin, a nonagrarian and trading religion; hardly a religion at all, but a result of secular ambition." This flaw engendered fatal results: "Because the South never created a fitting religion, the social structure of the South began grievously to break down two generations after the Civil War. . . ." To be blunt: Allen Tate opined that the Old South's gravest defect was that it was not Roman Catholic, a suggestion unpalatable even to Southern traditionalists at the tag-end of the most anti-Catholic decade in the region's history.

Tate's discomfiture had surfaced before 1930. In the midst of his embrace of self-conscious Southernism in the late '20s he had published what remains his most famous poem, "Ode to the Confederate Dead." The title is ironic; when Tate sent a draft to Donald Davidson, a shocked Davidson retorted: "And where, O Allen Tate, are the dead? You have buried them completely out of sight. . . ." From the perspective of Davidson, the most unyielding traditionalist among the Agrarians, that is precisely what Tate had done.

The poem is not about the heroic Confederate dead and the tradition they embodied, a tradition that Davidson would soon celebrate unambiguously in his poetic rejoinder to Tate, "Lee in the Mountains". Rather, the ode dissects the perplexity, confusion and solipsism of a young man of the 1920s, who stands by the gate of a Confederate cemetery contemplating "Row after row with strict impunity/The headstones. . . ." The observer admires the courage, fortitude and self-sacrifice of the slain warriors:

> Turn your eyes to the immoderate past,
> Turn to the inscrutable infantry rising
> Demons out of the earth . . .

But, he adds, "they will not last"—and neither will the tradition they exemplify. The young man wishes he could emulate

them, but the world has changed, the South has been transformed, and the old customs, mores and values are attenuated.

> What shall we who count our days and bow
> Our heads with a commemorial woe
> In the ribboned coats of grim felicity,
> What shall we say of the bones, unclean,
> Whose verdurous anonymity will grow?

The answer?

> We shall say only the leaves whispering
> In the improbable mist of nightfall
> That falls on multiple wing.

The Confederate dead return to the elements, and the young
Southerner is imprisoned in "mute speculation."

Near the end of "Remarks on the Southern Religion" Tate
poses a salient question: "How may the Southerner take hold
of his Tradition?" The succinct answer has baffled and be-
mused readers ever since: "by violence." That is exactly what
Tate attempted in the 1930s: by violent self-consciousness and
disciplined strategy to smash out of the solipsistic cage sur-
rounding the observer in the "Ode" and to seize the tradition
and make it his own.

There was another possibility, but to the Tate of 1930 it did
not constitute one of William James's "live options." After
the word "violence" in his essay, Tate set down two sentences
pregnant with meaning: "For this answer is inevitable. He
cannot fall back upon his religion, simply because it was
never articulated and organized for him. . . ." A year earlier
Tate had not been so willing to rule out religion. Writing to
Davidson from Paris, where Tate was enjoying a year abroad
on a Guggenheim Fellowship, he remarked: "I am more and
more heading towards Catholicism." In his reply Davidson
reproved his young friend for gloominess, and urged him not

to fall for the Catholic bait. Davidson admitted that he had
pondered the bait himself:

> I, too, am attracted somewhat toward Catholicism, as toward High
> Church Episcopalianism. But I like better to be tied up with no
> church at all. I find myself more repelled than attracted by all
> clergymen and priests. If it were not for them, possibly I could
> become something-or-other in a religious way. As matters stand,
> I seem to be bothered less by religious matters than by anything
> else.

Perhaps the old bugbear of priestcraft scared Tate off. In
any event, he resigned himself to the conclusion that, though
Protestantism offered nothing to the Southern traditionalist,
neither did Catholicism. For Tate, this signalled the beginning, not the end, of his spiritual struggle; unlike Davidson,
he was not "bothered less by religious matters than by anything else." For the rest of the 1930s he continued to grasp the
Southern tradition "by violence." By the end of the decade he
realized that it would not work.

In his sole novel, *The Fathers*, published in 1938, he returned to where he had begun with "Ode to the Confederate
Dead": the Yeatsean center would not hold; the rough beast
of modernity had slouched into Bethlehem and tradition was
powerless to master it. Something more was needed to give
meaning to existence. Tate never revealed in print the nature
of his journey in the 1940s, but one of immense magnitude it
surely was, for in 1950 he arrived in Rome. From then until his
death in 1979 he remained a Catholic, though—like Katherine Anne Porter, with whom he once had a brief fling—his
commitment to the Church struck some observers as problematic. In the last years of his life he returned to where it had
all begun: Nashville. Here he lay stricken with emphysema,
bedridden and waiting to die. Once a week a priest came to
give him the Eucharist, and when he finally died at the age
of seventy-nine, he received the last rites of the Church.

IX

The most notable convert in the next generation of Southern writers—those born in the 1910s and 1920s—is Walker Percy. That Percy traveled a different road to Rome than did Tate could possibly be attributed to the disparity in their ages: Percy, born in 1916, came to manhood in a different South than did Tate, born in 1899. But more than decades is involved. Percy's conversion does not fall neatly under the rubric of the search for a lasting tradition to replace the fallen South.

As a child, Percy suffered two devastating personal losses that made him acutely aware of the fragility of existence: his father committed suicide and several years later his mother died in an automobile crash. Walker and his two brothers were adopted and raised by their father's cousin, William Alexander Percy of Greenville, Mississippi.

Will Percy was in many ways the *beau ideal* of the old order. A Delta plantation-owner and lawyer, he exemplified the gentlemanly virtues cherished by the Old South. Handsome, courtly, gracious, hospitable, paternally benevolent to blacks, he represented the best of Southern tradition. Walker came of age under the tutelage of the man the Percy boys called "Uncle Will." Walker has never ceased to admire Will Percy and the Roman virtues he embodied, yet he never incorporated those attributes fully into himself. Unlike Tate, who longed to recapture the past, Walker Percy knew that it could not be restored, not by "violence" nor by any other means. Percy was a Southerner as surely as Tate was, but he was harbinger of today's Southerner—cut loose from tradition and forced to find the meaning of existence in a South that has come unmoored. His search took him first to psychoanalysis; while studying medicine at Columbia University he underwent a prolonged course of therapy. He turned next to existentialism, immersing himself in the European philosophers while recuperating from tuberculosis contracted during a residency in pathology at Bellevue Hospital.

Walker Percy's conversion to Catholicism in the late 1940s would have troubled Uncle Will, who had died in 1942. Will Percy's mother had been a Catholic and Will had been raised in the Church. In a fit of adolescent piety he had once even decided to become a priest. At the age of sixteen he had gone off to the University of the South at Sewanee, Tennessee, and there, as he later recounted in his autobiography, *Lanterns on the Levee*, he lost his faith. One Sunday morning he rode on horseback down the mountain to the local Catholic church in Winchester; by the time he got back to campus his faith had vanished. He wrote later:

> So I knelt in the little Winchester church examining my conscience and preparing for confession. How it came about did not seem sudden or dramatic or anything but sad. As I started to the confessional I knew there was no use going, no priest could absolve me, no church could direct my life or my judgment, what most I believed I could not believe.

Will Percy lived the rest of his days as a stoic, cultivating the virtues that had long enabled the Southern gentleman to order his life and the society around him. Walker Percy did not reject Uncle Will's code; he simply never possessed it—it was not an option to choose or to repudiate. Psychoanalysis and atheistic existentialism could not do for Walker what stoicism had done for his adoptive father. Catholicism did.

X

These conversions stand out for their very unusualness—not because the converts were famous writers, but because so few Southerners of any kind have turned to Rome in the twentieth century. Intensely anti-Catholic, militantly fundamentalist, the South has not been receptive to the Church's message. Those who have responded to it have trod a lonely path that has directed their footsteps away from solidarity with their region and their people. Perhaps writers figure so prominently in this phenomenon because they, in a sense, had already suffered alienation because of their devotion to art, a vocation never highly honored in the South. Once alienated for the sake of art, they perhaps found it easier to embrace an alien religion. But this is to engage in sociological and psychological reductionism, always a hazard in trying to fathom the motives of converts. The easiest—and also most mysterious—explanation is simply to say that the Spirit listeth where it will.

5. If Your Heart's Not in Dixie. . .

In *The Souls of Black Folk,* published in 1903, W. E. B. DuBois noted the "twoness" forced upon the black man: he was both *of* America and *not of* it, a marginal man caught between two identities. The Southern Catholic ought to understand this situation. He is a Southerner, but at the same time, something both more and less. Pickup trucks defiantly display a bumper-sticker that bears the message: "If your [a picture of a heart] is not in Dixie, then get your [drawing of the hind end of a mule] out." A Catholic cannot surrender his heart entirely to Dixie, for a part of it—the most important part—lies in Rome. Yet he loves the South, and because of this he experiences something akin to DuBois's "twoness."

This divided loyalty does not cause most Southern Catholics to suffer the omnipresent identity crisis of our era: Who am I? Cradle Catholics do not agonize over a dilemma; they seem to rest comfortably in both their Southernness and their Catholicism. This cradle Catholic, whose ancestry likely dates to the Irish and German immigration of the antebellum period, is certainly a Southerner, but he enjoys the added benefit of belonging to the nationwide community of German and Irish Americans. His "twoness" is more blessing than curse, for it provides him with two strong identities. The Southern cradle Catholic of English descent (and there are not many of them

left) is too far removed from his immigrant forebears to feel
an ethnic bond; he is, in this respect, more wholly Southern
than those of Irish or German extraction. He probably experiences no conflict between Southernness and Catholicity,
because both of these identities are rooted in the very origins
of the South.

The convert differs from these two groups. He is most likely
of English or Scotch-Irish ancestry, and because of this he
faces a troubling problem: he cannot trace his Catholicism to
roots in Maryland or Kentucky, and thereby meld Southernness and Catholicity into a comfortable unity. His ancestors
were Protestants, not Catholics. Nor can he link his religion
to Irish or German ethnicity and through this act tie himself
to a broader national community. The Southern convert finds
himself riven by the problem of "twoness."

In examining what it means to be a Catholic in the South
today, I write from the convert's perspective. Aside from my
personal situation, another reason persuades me to adopt this
angle of vision: the hope of Catholicism in the South lies with
the convert. The native cradle Catholic numbers too few of his
kind to determine the religious destiny of the region, and the
transplanted Yankee Catholic remains alien to the manners,
mores and traditions of his adopted homeland. I shall save my
speculations about the future of Catholicism in the South for
the concluding chapter. Here I wish to draw upon my own
experience as one who is both a Southerner and a convert.

II

In an odd way, it is good to live amidst the militant Protestants who dominate the South. They care intensely about
Christianity in a way that few other Americans do. They do
not treat it as a routine affair, and they are not ashamed to
own up to the fervency of their belief. There is nothing per-
functory about religion for these folks.

An orthodox Catholic shares a common language with
these people. As long as he refrains from broaching divisive
teachings he can agree upon much with his fundamentalist neighbors. To promote peaceful neighborly discourse the
Catholic must avoid a bevy of inflammatory topics: the papacy, the Virgin Mary, saints, purgatory, monks, nuns, clerical celibacy, confession, the Mass, biblical exegesis, the Protestant Reformation. What's left? More than one might guess.

The fundamentalist brooks no opposition to the divinity
of Christ or to the atoning, redemptive death of the Savior. He believes adamantly in the omnipotence, omniscience
and omnipresence of God. Though his biblical literalism in-
duces bizarre fantasies to racket around in his brain, he does
not equivocate on the holiness and divine inspiration of the
Bible. He rejects the idea of purgatory, but he believes in a
heaven and hell so real that it sounds as if he has visited both
places. He has no truck with watered-down notions of sin; he
knows that man is a fallen creature and that sin infects every
fiber of his being. He does not try to foist the blame for evil
onto society or impersonal historical forces. Theological liberalism has made inroads in the South, especially among the
clergy in the Methodist, Presbyterian and Episcopal churches,
but among the vast numbers of white and black Southerners,
neo-modernism is about as welcome as AIDS. Steer the conversation gingerly and one can talk with a fundamentalist.
Because of his Protestant background, the Southern convert
enjoys a decided advantage over other Catholics: he knows
the local patois.

The Southern Protestant scorns the Catholic's superstitions
and mystifications, but he has his own versions of these, and
this should endear him to the Catholic. The fundamentalist ridicules the notion that a dead saint's dried blood can
liquify, but he believes that God can make Cheryl Prewitt's
maimed leg grow. He scoffs at weeping statues of the Virgin,
but he relinquishes his skepticism when it comes to images of
Christ on upright freezers in Tennessee. Like the Catholic, he

credits miracles; he simply wants to pick and choose his own miraculous occurrences. Curiously enough, the charismatic Catholic—suspect in his own communion—finds boon companions among Southern pentecostals, who have been gabbling in tongues for close to a century.

A couple of years ago I visited a friend of mine who was then teaching at Christendom College, an orthodox Catholic institution located, improbably, in Front Royal, Virginia, an area not famed as a hotbed of Catholicism. My friend mentioned two problems at the college: acceptance by the local community and an infestation of snakes, the latter caused by construction projects that had disturbed the reptiles' nesting areas. As the hour lengthened and the level of liquor in the Jack Daniel's bottle receded, I hit upon a solution that addressed both difficulties at once: form a Catholic snake-handling sect and rename the school Tom Aquinas Bible College. Snakes and citizenry alike would be happy.

One needs a sense of humor when dealing with fundamentalists, but to be satisfied with laughing at them is to miss a vital point: much of what strikes Catholics (and most other Americans as well) as Southern goofiness is really only a distortion of historic Christian tenets. These people may have only one oar in the water, but at least they know what an oar is and where the water is located.

Take, for example, Arlene Gardner's "precious freezer" in Estil Springs. It is easy to mock Mrs. Gardner's credulity, and if the wire services picked up the story, it no doubt furnished an evening's entertainment for sophisticates in New York, Boston, Chicago and Los Angeles. But Arlene Gardner is serious; her childlike faith finds no difficulty in believing that Christ would manifest his presence on her freezer. In her own primitive way she acknowledges that the divine shatters mundaneness in the most startling manner. God's way is not man's, and man had best stand ready for surprises. Her God does not abide by the rules and logic of scientifically sophisticated, technologically advanced Western society. She

knows that the Spirit listeth where it will, and if it chooses
to swoop down upon a freezer in Tennessee, well, that is no
more bizarre than the infant-God lying in a manger in Bethlehem. As Walker Percy would say, Mrs. Gardner is onto something. Her fault lies not in her credulity but in her separation
from the counsel, support and guidance of a Church that can
structure and channel her fervency. Without this, she, like so
many Southerners, is a free-lance believer, prey to charlatans
and potential victim of her own extravagant piety.

III

Catholics no longer suffer from the cancerous bigotry that
infected the South earlier in this century. Anti-Catholicism
is no longer a creed among most Protestants. Southerners are
more accustomed to Catholics and more willing to grant their
religion a place as another denomination. Well, almost: to
be a Catholic has not yet attained the respectability that a
Methodist or Baptist commands.

That Catholics do not adhere to the same mores and stric-
tures that prevail in Protestant circles still causes problems.
In Protestant eyes, for example, Catholics are guilty of dangerous worldliness. Catholics drink, and in the land of fundamentalism, demon rum is a fierce stalker of godly souls.
The very idea of using wine in communion is shocking; no
wonder, the fundamentalist clucks, that so many priests suc-
cumb to alcoholism. A Protestant friend of mine attributed
this to the fact that priests begin each day with a belt of wine
in the Mass—one sip and down the chute you go. Smoking,
dancing, the use of make-up and jewelry—all those fleshly
things anathematized by God-fearing fundamentalists—strike
Catholics as less than sinful.

Some Southerners suspect that the heart of the Catholic
religion lies not in the Mass, but in the Wednesday-night

bingo game. Protestants flock to church on that evening for a mid-week prayer service; Catholics crowd into parish halls to gamble. Many are the jokes about Catholics and bingo. Most of them, of course, originate with Catholics and are passed on to Protestants. My favorite involves two soldiers— one from the North, the other from the South—who find themselves trapped in a foxhole in a decidedly life-threatening situation (any recent war will do). The Northerner, figuring that his companion is acquainted with the Lord, urges him to pray. Unfortunately, the Southerner happens to be one of those rare creatures from the Bible Belt who is unchurched. "Sorry," he says, "I ain't never been inside a church in my life." As circumstances grow more desperate, the Northern soldier frantically beseeches his friend to offer *some* kind of prayer. The Southerner wrings his brain and finally says: "I tell you what. I was raised in Atlanta next to a Catholic church. I used to hear them prayin' when the windows was open, and I think I can say one of them Catholic prayers." Relieved, his companion waits expectantly, only to hear the soldier begin to intone reverently, "Under the I, 7; under the O, 9. . . ."

Ignorance and misunderstanding of Catholicism are still rife below the Mason-Dixon line. Catholicism exudes a lingering scent of the strange and exotic. In good Southern fashion, I can best illustrate this with an anecdote. Nashville is home to an order of Dominican nuns. The convent is located near an office-complex known as Metro Center. On Saturdays and Sundays, when the center lies dormant, the nuns like to take their evening constitutional among the silent buildings and empty parking lots. As befits *Southern* nuns, they are quite traditional, a fact indicated by their long white habits. One Saturday evening a covey of nuns was strolling in Metro Center when two police cars roared up behind them, screeched to a halt and disgorged several officers. As the nuns turned toward the officers one of the policemen sheepishly apologized: "Sorry, ladies, somebody reported that the Klan was marching through Metro Center."

To point out that the South no longer seethes with animosity toward Catholicism is not to suggest that the old animus has vanished. It hasn't, though it is more subtle than blatant these days. It can be discerned in a certain intonation, in a slight arching of an eyebrow, in a veiled remark. My neighbor confronted me one day: "You're a Catholic, ain't ya?" "Why, yes," I replied, "how did you know?" "I seen you leaving mighty early on Sunday mornin's that's how." His remarks were ostensibly innocent enough, a harmless way of striking up a conversation. But there was a sly undercurrent beneath the surface cordiality; much that was thought, went unspoken. Perhaps it was the bluntness of his question, for in the South, blunt questions often lead to bloodshed. At the very least, they indicate poor breeding. Or maybe it was the special emphasis he placed upon the word *Catholic.* His intonation and demeanor disclosed the slightest of challenges, the merest hint that he had found me out in something.

I recently visited a priest I know in Lynchburg, Virginia. After Sunday Mass we went to Wendy's for hamburgers and french fries. Fr. Warner looked like a priest, for he was dressed in black and wearing a dog collar. As we sat down I glanced around at the other patrons. To my surprise, I caught several of them quickly averting their eyes after snatching a glimpse at us. At various times during our meal I noticed some of them surreptitiously peeking in our direction. Paranoia on my part? An overly active imagination? I think not—again, a matter of subtleties.

I suspect that it was not just the priest's presence that caught their attention, but my accompanying him. I do not look like the Southerner's notion of a Catholic, a creature who evokes in his mind something discernibly Irish, Slavic or Italianate in appearance. With my light-colored hair, blue eyes and Anglo features, I resemble the quintessential Southern WASP. Through the minds of those good Virginians ran something like this: "What's a nice Southern boy (contrary to what Yankees think, "boy" is not used solely to refer to elderly black

men) like that doing with a priest?" or "That priest is corrupt-
ing that boy!" When we finished eating, Fr. Warner reached
in his pocket for a pack of cigarettes: "I'm going to do what
I try not to do in public when I'm dressed this way." "What's
that?" I asked. "Smoke." Seeing my perplexity, he explained:
"It confirms all their worst suspicions about priests. They'll
expect me to pull out a bottle of whiskey next."

The Southern Catholic is familiar with another form of
asperity toward his Church. This one invariably begins with
the assertion: "Well, I believe everyone ought to be free to
worship as he sees fit, but. . . ." After the "but" follows a caveat,
a reservation of the type that would not be raised against, say,
a Baptist or Methodist. But: "I don't see why Catholics don't
let their priests marry." But: "How can Catholics believe in
something as crazy as purgatory?" But: "I think it's disgraceful
the way Catholics get drunk on Saturday night and then go to
church on Sunday morning." But: "Why do Catholics worship
Mary?" But: "Why are Catholics so hung-up on birth control?"
The Southern Catholic is acutely aware of that obtrusive "but"
that subverts the preceding avowal of tolerance.

I am a good friend to one of my wife's kinsmen, a man who
hasn't, as they say in the South, a mean bone in his body. He
knows that I am a Catholic (a perplexing oddity to him, I am
sure) and he would never deliberately say anything about my
religion to offend me, but sometimes he slips. Recently two
elderly cousins of his—widowed sisters with no children—had
to be placed in a nursing home. They, too, happen to be
Catholics. Like alcoholism and adultery, it occurs in the best
of families. "Their finances are a mess," he commented, "but
I reckon the priest will get all their money anyhow." He said
it unthinkingly, merely repeating, no doubt, what he had
heard all his life about the greed and chicanery of the Catholic
Church.

Two areas of the South—Florida and Texas—have in the
last two decades experienced a massive influx of immigrants:

Cubans and other Latins to Florida, Mexicans to Texas. This has created consternation among the natives, an anxiety that includes more than a tincture of anti-Catholicism, though that sentiment usually remains *sub rosa.* The issue for the native Southerner is not as acute in Florida as in Texas. The Latins have taken over *south* Florida, an area native Floridians—who live in the north of the state, from Jacksonville across to Panama City (the latter known affectionately as the "Redneck Riviera")—have always considered alien territory. Before the Cubans arrived, it was, they point out, infested with Jews from New York and New Jersey anyway.

Texans have no *cordon sanitaire* to protect them. As they see it, their whole state is being overrun by Mexicans. On the surface, the religious issue does not crop up. Talk with a Texan for awhile, however, and the truth will out. Not only is it those "goddamned" ("gosh-darned," if your informant is a Baptist) "Mexicans" that distress him, but those "goddamned Mexican *Catholics.*" One easily misses this aspect of the imbroglio, for the Texas Protestant, like his cousins elsewhere in the South, knows that it is not completely acceptable any longer—at least in polite company—to despise a man's religion.

IV

Lest these observations be taken as evidence of a convert's hypersensitivity, one should note that at times an anti-Catholicism worthy of the Golden Era of the '20s crawls out from under a rock. Jimmy Swaggart, the television evangelist in Baton Rouge, openly preaches his aversion for the Catholic Church. The archbishop of New Orleans has publically rebuked Swaggart—much, one might add, to the delight of Swaggart and his followers. Swaggart boasts immense popularity in the South; if anything, Southerners esteem him more than they do Pat Robertson or Jerry Falwell. Do the millions who watch his Bible-thumping evangelizing ignore his anti-Catholicism? Do they take it with a grain of salt, and chuckle at ol' Jimmy's antics? No. Swaggart's anti-Catholicism taps an underground reservoir and encourages his viewers to lower their buckets into it.

From 5:00 to 6:00 A.M. on weekday mornings one of the Nashville television stations airs a Bible-study program conducted by Swaggart, several of his clerical henchmen, and some of the professors from Swaggart's Bible college. Since prophetic interpretation plays an important part in the show, the old Whore of Babylon regularly puts in a titillating appearance. The pernicious teachings of the Catholic Church routinely come under fire. On one program, purgatory formed the topic of discussion. Swaggart and company treated viewers to a marvelous blend of ignorance, innuendo, half-truth and japery. Agreeing that no biblical justification exists for the doctrine, the assembled experts wrestled with the concept's provenance. One opined that Dante started the whole business with "that poem of his." Another suggested that ignorant medieval peasants, scared witless by the threat of hell-fire, forced the Church to establish a half-way house for departed sinners. In any event, they agreed, no Christian could believe such bosh.

Flagrant Catholic-baiting usually debouches not from the mainstream of Southern fundamentalism. Both Pat Robertson and Jerry Falwell, for example, eschew anti-popery as a way to rile the faithful. More often, this emanates from tiny fundamentalist sects, from store-front churches and cinder-block tabernacles, from shadowy, fly-by-night organizations that dote on conspiracies, plots and cabals. As Thomas Stritch suggests, the most vociferous anti-Catholicism is likely to be found on "the bottom rungs of southern Protestantism." Significantly, though, the Ku Klux Klan, a mere wraith compared to the Klan of the '20s, no longer seriously fosters pope-hating; Jews, blacks, Communists and secular humanists furnish enough anxiety to occupy the Klansman's febrile brain. Back in the 1970s the head of the Klan in Maryland was an Italian Catholic from Baltimore!

But the long-lived obsession with the Scarlet Woman will not die down among some groups. One of the most vicious of these—Tony Alamo's outfit—thrives in Nashville, where Alamo's crew runs a profitable Western-clothing store. Periodically, Alamo is hauled into court for some infraction, usually for violating labor laws; then he treats the city to a lugubrious tale of how Catholics are bent on silencing his ministry. Most Nashvillians laugh, or, because it has gotten so predictable, ignore the ruckus. But some listen: after all, at one time both the state's attorney and the sheriff of Davidson County were Catholics. Maybe they *are* out to get ol' Tony.

Several years ago Nashvillians awoke one morning to find the city covered with a blizzard of handbills; telephone poles, traffic signs, trash receptacles, abandoned buildings and automobile windshields were plastered with them. Alamo disclaimed responsibility, but it bore his marks. The scurrility of the missives amazed even veteran students of the genre. Oh, there was the tried-and-true: Lincoln and Garfield the victims of papal plots, and such. But there were new and startling twists. Pope John Paul is a homosexual who was once arrested for molesting small boys. Sigmund Freud converted to Catholicism and instructed the Church on how to use psychoanalysis to rid the world of the notion of sin. The Church controls the Mafia, the U.S. government and all the labor unions on earth. "The Vatican sponsors every major terrorist group in the world." That a terrorist attempted to assassinate the pope only proves how cleverly the Vatican disguises its designs and orchestrates its master strategy. For pure inventive genius, though, this one cannot be topped: "Jim Jones, a Roman Catholic Jesuit deacon posing as a Christian was sacrificed (not with poisoned Kool-aid), murdered, along with his flock by the Vatican to make the world look narrowly and suspiciously upon innocent Christian retreats." I am not certain what this means exactly, but it is a *tour de force* of anti-Catholic vitriol.

V

Admittedly, this sort of thing appears infrequently in the South these days; even many fundamentalists find it too rich to stomach. Oddly, though, at the same time that the scurrilous variety of anti-Catholicism is waning, another type is on the rise. Thirty years or so ago the most hardened Catholic-hater would at least begrudgingly admit that the American Church staunchly opposed Communism. After all, wasn't Joe McCarthy a good Catholic? Then, too, no more adamantly anti-Communist patriot lived than Cardinal Spellman. Alas, the Southern Catholic no longer receives congratulations from conservative patriots for belonging to a Church that helps to thwart the Red Menace.

Among right-wing Southerners the Catholic Church is now indicted as *part of* the Red Menace. "The pope is a socialist," one hears. The Southerner watches television and reads the newspaper, and he is aware of the bishops' pacifistic statements on war and their pinkish pronouncements on the economy and social justice. He hears about Marxist Jesuits in the United States, revolutionary priests in Nicaragua and liberation theologians in Brazil. Nuns were mysterious and slightly scary when they were immured in convents, but now they pop up on the six o'clock news to advocate abortion, assail the boys in uniform and denounce free-enterprise. At one time, Southerners had to divide their hatred between leftists and Catholics; now they can combine the two aversions. The Southern Catholic finds himself doubly damned, his politics as suspect as his religion.

VI

If the Southerner dislikes the Church's stand on social justice and war and peace, other "Catholic" issues elicit a mixed
response from him. I am uncertain whether the Catholic position on birth control, abortion and federal aid to parochial
schools exacerbates ancestral animosities toward the Church,
or if, perhaps, it lessens tensions and promotes a more benevolent attitude among Protestants. These issues cut in a number
of different directions.

The Church's stance on birth control probably bemuses
Southerners, rather than evoking strong feelings one way or
the other. For most Southerners, this issue does not clamor
for debate. Most of them belong to denominations that long
ago jettisoned opposition to birth control, or to ones that have
never enunciated an official policy on the subject. I suspect
that most fundamentalists think that the less said publically
about sex, the better. They are a tad squeamish about open
talk of bedroom matters, although, contrary to what liberals
say, they do not necessarily seethe with sexual neuroses. With
their rural background, they tend toward an earthiness about
sex; they do not—unlike liberated New Yorkers—provide psychiatrists with a handsome income to straighten out their sex
life.

Yuppieism and moral relativism have both slithered into
the South in recent years, and among adherents of these
creeds there exists irritation at the Church's opposition to
"family planning," as they say euphemistically at Planned
Parenthood. Such people, found increasingly in the posh
suburbs of major Southern cities, twitter about "quality of
life," and more babies mean, to them, less quality. They
harbor deep anxieties over the pullulating masses in Latin
America, Africa and Asia. Can't the Church see that birth
control is the only solution? they plaintively ask.

When fundamentalists manage to discern the connection

between birth control and rampant sexual promiscuity it casts the Catholic Church in a more favorable light; at times the Church's opposition to sexual libertarianism and the more bizarre forms of sex education even elicits a smidgen of admiration from fundamentalists. Here the fundamentalist perceives the Church as . . . well, not exactly an *ally,* but at least as fighting the right enemies.

Southerners have aroused themselves belatedly over the abortion issue. Strong opinions on this now circulate in the South, and voices are occasionally raised in anger. This intensity of feeling cuts both ways when the Southerner ponders the Church's adamancy. Educated and prosperous Southerners (those, in other words, most like their counterparts in the North) tend to dislike what they type as "extremists" on both sides of the fight. Feminism does not wash in the South, so the Southerner is unsympathetic with the woman's-right justification of abortion. But this prosperous and enlightened Southerner does not cotton to religious fanatics either. He likely takes what he considers a "moderate" position: abortion ought not to be practiced casually, but it is warranted in some cases. Also, he has imbibed enough of the relativism of our age to feel uneasy at forcing people to abide by moral prescriptions. "Live and let live," he says, without recognizing the brutal irony this statement conveys when it comes to abortion. The feminists are loopy fanatics, he agrees, but then, the Catholic Church exudes its own brand of fanaticism, a kind that evokes images of medieval intolerance and the auto-da-fé.

Fundamentalists love to denounce the Catholic Church for intolerance; a virtuoso preacher can make your skin crawl with a graphic description of flames licking at the flanks of a Protestant martyr. But something else distresses the fundamentalist: he finds it hard to blink the horror of a million and a half abortions a year. His clerical media-heroes—Robertson, Falwell, Swaggart—denounce abortion unequivocally, and an increasing number of local pastors have joined the anti-abortion ranks. The Southern

fundamentalist conscience has awakened. On no other issue
does the Catholic Church benefit so much in the eyes of fundamentalists, for with all Rome's faults, it has, they admit,
led the fight against this evil. Here lies the most promising
opportunity for Southern Catholics and fundamentalists to
reach across the gulf that separates them. I myself have seen
in Nashville an anti-abortion picket line that included both
a tiny, fully-habited nun and a strapping, broad-shouldered
pentecostal preacher.

Because of the Southerner's devotion (as he sees it) to the
principle of church-state separation, he has always denounced
the Catholic Church's efforts to tap the public till to support parochial education. Ironically, at the very moment when
Catholics seem less exercised over this issue, the Southern
Protestant—especially the fundamentalist—is more receptive
to the idea; that is, if the government includes Protestant
schools in its largesse. The reason is easy to figure: in the
last two decades church schools have sprouted in the South
like kudzu on a steamy July afternoon. One hates to deprive
liberals of their prejudices, but this proliferation has little
to do with race. It represents the fundamentalists' response
to the decline of rigor, discipline and morality in the public schools. Although they remain wary of direct federal aid
(knowing that with the money come the bureaucrats), most of
them, I believe, would welcome relief in the form of tax credits or vouchers. Suddenly, the Catholic position looks more
like common sense and less like a Rome-inspired plot to un-
dermine democracy and destroy the public schools. Financial
exigency, like politics, can make strange bedfellows.

VII

The inevitable question: Wouldn't I be happier living elsewhere, in a place with a greater density of Catholics? Since
the faith matters above all else, wouldn't it make sense to

dwell among fellow believers, to live somewhere that boasted a Catholic church on every corner instead of a Baptist or Methodist one? The answer is easy: No. Although I share a common belief with Catholics, I am not attuned to their culture, an ethos shaped largely by the immigrant-urban experience of the North. I am a Southerner, and this land is bred in the marrow of my bones. As the Agrarians of the 1930s said, echoing an old song, "In Dixieland I'll take my stand."

One returns to DuBois's concept of "twoness." The white South forced this bifurcation upon the black man, but mine is voluntary, and the South does not look kindly upon such a choice. Love it or leave it: no intermediate categories. This attitude derives from the heavy historical burden the Southerner has lugged around with him. Since the 1830s he has been required to assert his solidarity with his region in defiance of external threats.

In the antebellum era the abolitionist crusade and growing sectional estrangement encouraged him to circle the wagons, to retreat within the concentric circles of region, state, locality, kith and kin. The crushing defeat of 1865 tightened these bonds. Reconstruction demanded unity to expel the Yankees and to regain self-determination. In the years after Reconstruction the necessity to establish a new *modus vivendi* in race relations required white solidarity, as Tom Watson discovered to his chagrin.

In the decades following World War One the South's ignorance, backwardness, poverty and extravagant religiosity made it both a shame and a laughingstock to the rest of America. Wounded by these barbs, the Southerner took refuge in the bosom of his benighted homeland. In the early 1960s the civil rights movement provoked him to an anger and defensiveness he had not displayed so intensely since the Civil War. In the late '60s his futile support of the war in Vietnam earned him additional contempt from enlightened folk outside the South; James Calley, the butcher of Mylai, he was constantly reminded, was from Georgia. The white Southerner did not much warm to Jimmy Carter, but he was glad to see one of his own in the White House again. He noted bitterly that Carter's downfall, though self-induced, brought renewed mockery of things Southern. For a century and a half, then, the Southerner has vested his faith in regional solidarity; to betray that, was to betray all he cherished.

Prosperity, the rise of the Sun Belt and Ronald Reagan's eight years in the White House have assuaged the white Southerner's defensiveness and encouraged him to view himself as the quintessential American. In some ways, this new optimism makes it easier to be a Catholic in the South, for in Reagan territory, prosperity and patriotism, not religion, tend to measure the man. But I do not wish to be accepted because my Catholicism is of little consequence. And, of course, it isn't; where religion is concerned, the Southerner is still likely to place a premium upon Protestant solidarity.

VIII

The Southern Catholic—especially the convert—finds himself in an enviable position. To call him a marginal man is to assert a partial truth; another perspective recognizes that his marginality—his "twoness," if you will—permits him to enjoy the best of both worlds. To live in the South and to define oneself solely as a Catholic is to doom oneself to narrowness. It promotes disdain for the particularities of time, place and circumstance: O, Lord, let me hurry through this world so I can get to heaven where there won't be any Jesus-screaming fundamentalists, Ku Kluxers, flag-waving neo-Confederates, New-South Babbitts in polyester suits, or cretinous rednecks.

By the same token, *not* to be a Catholic in the South makes it too easy to luxuriate in the cocoon of culture. The Southern Protestant easily falls captive to this culture, for the Southern churches have never been noted for their resistance to the claims of society. Instead of Jeremiah, we have Jerry Falwell;

instead of Isaiah, Pat Robertson; instead of Ezekiel, Jimmy Swaggart—all of whom apotheosize the South as the highest embodiment of Christian civilization.

To be both a Southerner and a Catholic is to be granted a unique angle of vision. Both fully Southern and fully Catholic: a great mystery, that, but a privileged position to occupy. I *am* a Southerner: my people settled in Maryland and Virginia before the Revolution; they held slaves; they fought for the South at Manassas and Fredericksburg, at Sharpsburg and Gettysburg, at Chancellorsville and Seven Forks. Mostly Methodists, they worshiped with millions of their fellow Southerners. For centuries, they tilled the soil, raised families, feared God, cherished hearth and home, kith and kin, and bequeathed to their progeny the traditions of the land they loved. At the risk of sounding prideful, I will match my Southern credentials against those of any Baptist from Mississippi or Methodist from Georgia.

I *am* a Catholic. I forsook fundamentalism and anti-Catholicism to become one, but I did not forsake the South. I did, however, transfer my *ultimate* loyalties to Rome, and in doing so, I accepted the fact that my fellow Southerners would not understand, and might even be a bit miffed at me. I am as fully Catholic in religion (though not in culture) as any Irish-American from Boston, Italian-American from the Bronx, or Polish-American from Chicago.

As a Southerner I am rooted in time, place and circumstance. The world's body, in all its specificity, concreteness and particularity, is a gift to me from my homeland. Its traditions are mine, in so far as those traditions have survived the acids of modernity. I am part of a web of existence that weaves past to present, present to future. I have a place where I belong. To be a Southerner is not an invitation to misery.

But the supreme joy comes not from my Southernness, but from Catholicism. This suffuses my existence with transcendence and extends to me—a broken, fallen creature—the promise of eternal life. It does not demand that I repudiate the South; it reveals, rather, that the South I love—the people, the land, the traditions—is part of God's created order, part of the goodness that comes from the hand of the creator. It encourages me to love this piece of creation, but not to love it too dearly, not to elevate it above all else or to transmogrify it into an idol. Catholicism gives me an outside standard with which to judge my homeland. It cautions me not to judge too harshly, for without God's irruption into man's time, there can be no perfect order on this earth. But it reminds me also that because man's world is flawed, I must be willing to discern the South's shortcomings.

The Catholic Church enables me to see that, through some mystery of providence, I was born into the South of the mid-twentieth century, and that it is my appointed task to be a Southerner and a Catholic in this time and place. My true home, the heart's own country, lies elsewhere: "beyond the region of thunder," as a favorite prayer of Flannery O'Connor's says, "in a land that is always peaceful, always serene and bright with the resplendent glory of God." A land, one might add, where there is neither Greek nor Jew, Northerner nor Southerner, Catholic nor Protestant.

6. A Catholic South?

Whatever the prospects for Catholic gains in the South, the pope's visit to Dixie in September 1987 did not enhance them. His stop in New Orleans was appropriate, for it confirmed that city's stature as a historic center of American Catholicism, but why, pray tell, did he bother with South Carolina, where the state's entire Catholic population could fit comfortably into the University of South Carolina's football stadium? As for Miami, to call it a "Southern" city would be to stretch the term to meaninglessness; one might as well include Indianapolis or Phoenix as part of the South. Somebody in the Vatican blew it, missing the potential symbolism of the pope's trip; the Holy Father needs a new PR staff.

Where would I have sent the pope? He would have begun his tour at St. Mary's City, Maryland, and there, at the birthplace of Catholicism in the South, he would have celebrated a Mass to recall the heroism of that first lonely band of Catholics, and to herald the future increase of the flock in the South. From there, Pope John Paul would have journeyed the short distance to Baltimore, seat of the first bishop in the United States and, until our own century, the queen city of the Church in America.

Leaving Baltimore, he would have swung down to Richmond. Richmond? Yes, because here I have in mind an act rich with symbolism, for a papal visit would have reminded Southerners that (as Allen Tate and others discovered), with the fall of the Confederacy, only Rome offers an adequate foundation for belief and commitment to a people schooled in tradition. From Richmond the pope would have crossed the Appalachian Mountains to the village of Bardstown, Kentucky, site of the first bishopric in the western part of the South, and the second historic locus of Southern Catholicism. I would have kept New Orleans on the itinerary; it is, after all, the third great center of Catholicism in the South.

Then I would have sent the pope to one last place: Atlanta. Here I would have had him perform a rite of exorcism upon the city that represents the misguided course Southerners have steered since World War Two. Atlanta is the capital of the New South; with its glitter, arrogance, hedonism and worship of mammon, it exemplifies the soulless mediocrity of the Sun Belt. After the pope left Atlanta, I would have sat back and watched the media and the citizens of the South fulminate over the pope's symbolically astute invasion of Dixie. It would have been fun to watch Jimmy Swaggart gnash his teeth.

II

Alas, one cannot fault the Vatican for failing to solicit my advice; in worldwide perspective, the Catholic community of the South is too minuscule to warrant much attention from the Holy Father. That the pope should visit here at all is of immense significance. On the Vatican's maps the South must be labeled "Hostile Territory," or at least, "Terra Incognita." Outside of, say, the Soviet Union or Iran, one can imagine few places less receptive to a visit from the Roman pontiff. This is mission territory, and if that spells vast opportunity, it also indicates a land of incorrigible resistance to the invitation to commune with Rome.

The Catholic community will expand as more migrants

pour into the land of sunshine and jobs. But this increase will be far outstripped by the multitudes of Protestants and the unchurched who head south. If the Church counts on migratory Yankees to swell its numbers, it is consigning Catholicism to permanent numerical insignificance in the South. Since the native Catholic population is small, that leaves large-scale conversion as the hope. To be blunt: it ain't a-goin' to happen. The South is—and will remain—the most thoroughly Protestant region of the United States. The waning of old-style anti-Catholicism does not mean that Southerners will become more receptive to the Catholic message; if the area is less anti-Catholic, it is no less pro-Protestant. The Southern wings of the mainline churches—Methodist, Presbyterian and Episcopal—continue to lose numbers. This leakage does not redound to the benefit of the Catholic Church. My guess is that when someone leaves one of these bodies he goes in one of two directions: either he joins one of the thriving fundamentalist denominations, or he becomes a nominal Christian, listed on no one's rolls. This latter category promises to grow as secularization plies its trade in the South.

What makes the South so hard a nut to crack is not simply that it is Protestant, but that it is defiantly fundamentalist. Save for Methodism, the churches that dominate the region are growing, not declining. The Southern Baptist Convention, with fourteen and a half million members (and they do not count children until they are baptized between the ages of about nine to twelve), is the largest Protestant denomination in America. It exercises a powerful sway in the South. It offers the loose ecclesiological structure, Bible-based message and emotional satisfaction that huge numbers of Americans crave. It enjoys something of the stature of an established church, shaping as it does the popular religious ethos and providing Southerners with a model of successful, vibrant Protestantism.

The Assemblies of God—the body that defrocked Jim Bakker and, more recently, the Rev. Swaggart—boasts one of the highest annual rates of membership gain of any denomination in the country. It thrives in the South, its charismatic fervency filling the emotional void that Americans discern in their lives. The Church of Christ, a more fundamentalist faith than does not exist, has recently turned to serious evangelism, a practice it formerly eschewed because it could count upon inherited loyalty. Its new activism will make it even more formidable. Small, but dynamic denominations such as the Jehovah's Witnesses and Seventh-Day Adventists have chalked up impressive gains in the South, and the Mormons have turned the region into a ripe mission field. Finally, millions of Southerners belong to independent fundamentalist churches, bodies that spring up faster than one can tally.

The primary attraction of these churches is the exact opposite of what the Catholic Church offers. Their appeal is to the Bible and the heart, areas in which Catholicism finds it difficult to compete. Not only do they revere the Bible as the *only* foundation of the faith, but they have little problem with the sort of scholarship that undermines biblical authority. If heresy flares up, they quickly snuff it out; dissent does not flourish in these churches, and they—unlike Catholics—are not afraid to call heresy by its right name. Because of their biblical literalism, they maintain a doctrinal certitude that post-Vatican II Catholicism, swarming with revisionism, doubt and questioning, cannot match. A Charles Curran or Daniel Maguire would find himself expelled with alacrity from many Southern denominations.

Most of the churches that flourish in the South are congregational in polity. The source of this loose organization and fierce democracy probably lies most directly in the frontier conditions that spawned Southern revivalism, but for whatever reasons, Southerners do not take to the hierarchical structure of Catholicism. To their way of thinking, it infringes upon "soul liberty." Their emotionalism and warmth of fellowship also preclude any swing to Catholicism; the Catholic Church strikes them as cold and ritualistic, as a mere form of religion and not a vital, active gathering of believers.

The premillennialism so popular among Southerners provides assurance and meaning to a people living in troubled times. The Catholic interpretation of past, present and future seems a weak scheme to people imbued with the urgency of the premillennial world view. Their belief in the onrush of events toward the Second Coming makes the Catholic faith look like a sluggish, complacent compromise with the status quo. At a time when the Catholic Church focuses on social and economic issues and speaks little of eternal life, the Southern churches hold up a promise of the end of this groaning creation and an imminent return of the Lord that will shatter man's schemes for social and economic melioration.

The South's blacks, despite the demoralizing effects of their move to the region's cities, are every bit as religious as the whites. Their attachment to political liberalism, especially in the form of civil rights and federal anti-poverty programs, is deceptive; they share more with their conservative white brothers than either would like to admit. The same reasons that deter a white turn toward Rome prevent blacks from embracing Catholicism. In this respect, white and black Southerners present a unified front that Catholicism cannot expect to penetrate substantially. Black and white alike, the South is Protestant, and barring some change of a magnitude inconceivable, it will remain so.

III

Catholics should not despair. Oddly enough, these sometimes crazed Southern fundamentalists are potentially the best allies that orthodox Catholics have on the American religious scene. Some Catholics have interpreted Vatican II's opening to the world as an injunction to cozy up to Episcopalians, Unitarians, Quakers and the most liberal elements in the Lutheran, Methodist and Presbyterian denominations. This is ecumenism on the cheap, for it is painless: mix tepid theol-

ogy, sentimental humanitarianism and left-wing politics, and
voila!—We are all brothers in Christ.

Ecumenism counts only where each group holds firmly to
its own doctrinal commitments, but within this framework
seeks to improve relations with other Christians by exploring
points of agreement. Here lies an arduous, but potentially re-
warding, field of endeavor for Southern Catholics: to open
diplomatic relations with Baptists, pentecostals, the Church
of Christ and other fundamentalist denominations. This can
be accomplished only if Catholics respect the fundamentalists'
fervency and doctrinal certitude. Southern fundamentalists
are unreceptive to such overtures, but it behooves Catholics,
as members of the Mother Church, to take the initiative, to
weather rebuffs and to persist in efforts to form bonds of Christian fellowship. One caveat: the orthodox Catholic must not
seek agreement based on admiration of fundamentalists' penchant for right-wing politics. Such action would only repli-
cate on the right side of the spectrum what liberal Catholics
are engaged in on the left. Both activities cheapen the gospel
and tie the Church to temporal ends.

IV

Catholics need not be glum for another reason. The Church
continues to win souls in the South, and though their number
is not great, the quality is high. I do not suggest that converts
should be graded according to criteria—wealth, education,
social standing—that would elevate a college professor above
a plumber, a bank president above a farmer, a poet above a
housewife. The gospel knows no such distinctions; each soul
is uniquely priceless and valuable in the eyes of God. What I
mean is this: throughout the twentieth century the Church
has demonstrated a particular attraction for the brightest,
most talented and thoughtful Southerners. These people are
important, not because they are more meritorious, but because

of the influence they can exert in bringing others to the faith. A Catholic-convert professor in a Southern university, for example, is blessed with an exceptional opportunity to witness for the Church. A converted writer possesses the ability to fashion his art, not into religious propaganda, but into a monument to God's glory. One wonders how many souls have been led to the Church by reading Walker Percy's novels.

Such Southerners continue to find the Church. In 1977 Sheldon Vanauken published a book that ranks high among Southern literary endeavors of the past decade. In *A Severe Mercy*, the story of his Oxford years and of his beloved wife Davy's tragic death, Vanauken penetrated to the heart of the difficulty of following Christ in a world drenched with sadness and suffering. Vanauken was an Episcopalian, having entered that church in part because of the influence of C. S. Lewis. Davy died in the 1950s; Vanauken was bereft, and to fill the void he plunged into the social protest of the 1960s and flirted with the drug culture.

He returned to the Episcopal Church in the 1970s, but as the decade brought increasing chaos to this communion, he began to cast his eyes toward Rome. Reluctantly: too much of his past and present, his memories, friendships and ancestral ties, were bound up with the Episcopal communion for him to abandon it lightly. Finally in 1981, after several years of intellectual and emotional struggle, Vanauken, as he puts it, "crossed the English Channel" and headed for Rome. He has emerged as one of the most effective apologists for the faith, not only in the South, but in America at large. My grandmother, a rock-ribbed fundamentalist, used to say that when we arrive in heaven Christ will present us to those whom we have won to the kingdom. I am certain that a sizable company will be on hand to greet Sheldon Vanauken.

William P. Anderson, Jr., teaches sociology at Grove City College in Pennsylvania. He was born and raised in Memphis, Tennessee, and like so many Southerners over the past two hundred years, he grew up a Methodist. Anderson wore his Methodism lightly, and when he got to college in the mid-1970s he quickly discarded it for Marxism. And this at a Methodist college in West Tennessee. Upon graduating from college in 1978 he headed for the University of Connecticut to pursue doctoral studies. A strange thing happened: he repudiated Marxism; "strange," because by the late 1970s graduate students in sociology did not do that sort of thing. He returned to the Methodist church and mulled the idea of becoming a preacher.

In an article published recently in the *Homiletic and Pastoral Review*, Anderson recounts what happened next: "doubt, rather than certainty dogged me." The seed of Catholicism, planted a year or so earlier by a booklet from the Knights of Columbus, began to push its way above the soil of his soul. Against his better judgment, he moved fitfully down the road to Rome. Doubt warred with a longing to believe, as he underwent instruction and wrestled with a decision that refused to let him rest. Finally, he writes, "my heart quietly gave its assent," and on April 21, 1984, at the Easter Vigil Mass, he entered the Church.

Like William Anderson, Robert Bell (in this case a pseudonym) was raised in the Methodist church, a faith his ancestors had professed for generations. Like Anderson, too, Bell did not absorb Methodism at the depths of his soul. One was a Methodist because one's family and friends were Methodists, not because one had experienced the soul-shivering assault of Truth. An outstanding student in Nashville's most prestigious private school, Bell left home in the 1970s to attend an Ivy League university. Here he discovered Nietzsche, and the old German God-hater quickly cleansed him of the lingering traces of his childhood religion. Bell exulted in his newfound freedom from superstition, and along with this he jettisoned the tattered remnants of Christian morality he had carried with him to the East. There followed one of those seasons of sin that brings such delight to the flesh, but ultimately—if one is lucky—desolation to the soul. Nietzsche, sex and alcohol buoyed him on a wave of ecstasy, until the tide receded and left him beached.

His first gropings toward redemption came through a chance reading of Fr. Ronald Knox's *The Belief of Catholics,* a book that by the 1970s most American Catholics viewed as outmoded, a remnant of the bad old days before the Second Vatican Council. Bell found the book wonderfully *outré,* so far out of step with modern secular culture as to be fascinating. The more he read, the more Fr. Knox's words mysteriously rang with truth, a sound that resonated through his hollow soul. Slowly he dug his way out of the debris and limped to Rome, yet another Southern pilgrim who had arrived at his destination.

Notice that in each of these cases the individual found his own way into the Church. He was not badgered, pursued or proselytized by Catholics. The Church does not beat the bushes in the South to see how many souls it can bag. It waits, doors open, for them to wander in; it knows it has what they need. Carson McCullers, the Georgia novelist, and another of Flannery O'Connor's Christ-haunted souls, once recounted an incident from her childhood that illustrates this perfectly. She and her nurse were walking past a convent in McCullers's hometown of Columbus, Georgia. On this particular day the gates to the grounds were open, and young Carson peered in to see a group of children eating ice-cream cones and playing. In an essay that was not published until after McCullers's death, she recalled the experience:

> I watched fascinated. I wanted to go in, but my nurse said no, I was not Catholic. The next day, the gate was shut. But, year by year, I thought of what was going on, of this wonderful party, where I was shut out. I wanted to climb the wall, but I was too little. I beat on the wall once, and I knew all the time that there was a marvelous party going on, but I couldn't get in.

There *is* a party going on within the Church, and though the gates to the convent in Columbus, Georgia, were closed to the child Carson McCullers, the metaphorical gates are always open, waiting for those restless, discontented Southern souls to walk through and join the party. Sadly, McCullers herself never made it.

V

I had intended to call this book *The Black Pope from Mississippi*. But I decided against it when I realized that such an enigmatic title would needlessly perplex Catholic and Protestant readers alike. In Catholic parlance, "the black pope" is the head of the Society of Jesus; obviously the Jesuits have never chosen a general from Mississippi, so this offers no clue. The Protestant reader interprets "black" as "Negro" and comes up with the startling idea of a Negro pope from the Baptist-Methodist stronghold of Mississippi. Absurd, no? No: that is exactly what I have in mind.

I have a fantasy that I like to toy with. On those rare occasions when the perfect mood is upon me—when a particular conjunction of midnight hour, good Tennessee whiskey, and Southern brooding occurs—I envision a future South far different from the one I know. This South will have acquired what Allen Tate contended that the Old South most lacked: Catholicism.

Somehow, all those maniacal white fundamentalists and Jesus-shouting blacks will have found their way to Rome. Don't ask how; I am engaged in fantasizing, not in mapping a program of missionizing. At long last, the racial wounds will have healed, and the South's Catholic churches (far more numerous than the handful of Baptist and Methodist congregations that remain active as reminders of the region's distant Protestant past) will be filled to bursting with blacks and whites who mingle without a moment's thought. Martin Luther King, Jr.'s, "dream" will have come true, though not exactly in the way he supposed. The spiritual leader of the South will be the archbishop of Jackson, Mississippi, a black man who was born and raised on a farm. When St. Peter's throne falls open, speculation over who will be the next pope will include this great spiritual figure from the most Catholic region of the United States. This will not seem strange, for the college of cardinals will have already, in recent times, chosen popes from Brazil, Nigeria and the Philippines. When the papal electors emerge from a lengthy convocation, they will announce that the archbishop from Mississippi has been selected as the next Holy Father.

I am no prophet, so I refrain from insisting upon the prospects of this fantasy being translated into reality. But as all Southerners will admit, the Spirit listeth where it will and God's grace can shatter the most obdurate of certitudes. Since I am sure that God has a sense of humor, he may well be chuckling right now over the surprises he has in store for the land of Tom Watson and Frank Norris, of the Klan and hardcore fundamentalists, of Jerry Falwell and Jimmy Swaggart. Impossible! Impossible? Impossible. . . . *But!**

*P.S. The pope recently appointed a new archbishop of Atlanta. He is from Mississippi—he is black. Keep an eye on him.

Debts and Acknowledgments

When I departed the academic world in 1981, after ten years of teaching, I vowed never again to use a footnote or any of the other paraphernalia of what passes in the university for "scholarship." I had grown cynical about pedantry and inanition that disguise themselves in the garb of true scholarly endeavor. Still, no writer works in a vacuum; either directly or indirectly, he draws upon the information, insights and wisdom he has gleaned from others. In recognition of my own indebtedness, I wish to acknowledge the books (aside from those already mentioned by title in the text) that have aided me.

If I were forced to single out one volume as preeminent in molding my thinking about the South, it would be C. Vann Woodward's *The Burden of Southern History* (Louisiana State University Press, 1960). Although I disagree at times with Woodward, this book hovers over everything I write about the South. In all his books, Professor Woodward elevates scholarship into high art.

Although much has been written on the history of Catholicism in America, little attention has focused on the Church in the South. Catholic historians tend not to be attracted to the South, and Southern historians are uninterested in Catholicism. In searching for information about Southern Catholicism, I found the following especially useful: John J. Delaney, *Dictionary of American Catholic Biography* (Doubleday, 1984); Henry Warner Bowden, *Dictionary of American Religious Biography* (Greenwood Press, 1977); and Thomas Stritch, *The Catholic Church in Tennessee: The Sesquicentennial Story* (Nashville Catholic Center, 1987). Most of my biographical sketches are based on these books, especially John Delaney's.

Fr. Cornelius J. Buckley's *A Frenchman, A Chaplain, A Rebel: The War Letters of Pére Louis-Hippolyte Gache, S. J.* (Loyola University Press, 1979), reveals the trials and tribulations of a priest in the service of the Confederacy. Randall M. Miller and Jon L. Wakelyn (eds.), *Catholics in the Old South: Essays on Church and Culture* (Mercer University Press, 1983), not only contains much valuable information, but also points the right direction for future studies. For a broad overview of the history of Catholicism in America, I consulted Jay P. Dolan's *The American Catholic Experience* (Doubleday, 1985), a tendentious, but provocative book.

Much of the material on anti-Catholicism, especially on the early twentieth century, comes from research I did back in the late 1960s for my doctoral dissertation at the University of Virginia. This study was published in revised form as *Tried as by Fire: Southern Baptists and the Religious Controversies of the 1920s* (Mercer University Press, 1982). In addition to examining anti-Catholicism, this volume dissects Baptist thinking on evolution, premillennialism, biblical criticism, the Social Gospel, the rural-urban conflict and the presidential campaign of 1928.

In *The Persistent Prejudice: Anti-Catholicism in America* (Our Sunday Visitor, Inc., 1984), Michael Schwartz provides a militant Catholic perspective on the problem. The book is useful both for the history of anti-Catholicism and for its observations on the contemporary scene. C. Vann Woodward's *Tom Watson, Agrarian Rebel* (Macmillan, 1938) supplied material on the Georgia Populist. I found the episode involving Hugo Black in Gerald T. Dunne, *Hugo Black and the Judicial Revolution* (Simon and Schuster, 1977).

For the chapter on conversion I used the following books on Southern writers: Robert Bain, Joseph M. Flora and Louis D. Rubin, Jr. (eds.), *Southern Writers: A Biographical Dictionary* (Louisiana State University Press, 1979); Joan Givner, *Katherine Anne Porter: A Life* (Simon and Schuster, 1982); Dotson Rader, *Tennessee: Cry of the Heart* (Doubleday, 1985); Dakin Williams and Shepherd Mead, *Tennessee Williams: An Intimate Biography* (Arbor House, 1983); Donald Spoto, *The Kindness of Strangers: The Life of Tennessee Williams* (Little, Brown, 1985); John Tyree Fain and Thomas Daniel Young (eds.), *The Literary Correspondence of Donald Davidson and Allen Tate* (University of Georgia Press, 1974); William Rodney Allen, *Walker Percy: A Southern Wayfarer* (University Press of Mississippi, 1986); and Lewis A. Lawson and Victor A. Kramer (eds.), *Conversations with Walker Percy* (University Press of Mississippi, 1985).

Robert H. Brinkmeyer, Jr.'s, *Three Catholic Writers of the Modern South: Allen Tate, Caroline Gordon, Walker Percy* (University Press of Mississippi, 1985) deserves special commendation. This is a path-breaking study that warrants a reading by everyone interested in Catholicism and Southern literature.

The quotation from Carson McCullers that appears in chapter six comes from Virginia Spencer Carr, *The Lonely Hunter: A Biography of Carson McCullers* (Doubleday, 1975).

Along with Vann Woodward, Flannery O'Connor is never far from my thoughts when I contemplate the South. In this book I quote from her letters, collected in *The Habit of Being* (Farrar, Straus, Giroux, 1979), edited by Sally Fitzgerald. O'Connor's *Mystery and Manners: Occasional Prose* (Farrar, Straus, Giroux, 1961), edited by Sally and Robert Fitzgerald, informs all my thinking about Catholicism in the South.

Those who wish to delve further into my personal wrestlings with Catholicism and the South can do so with my spiritual autobiography, *Fleeing the Whore of Babylon: A Modern Conversion Story* (Christian Classics, Inc., 1986).